BIG PIT SILVERDALE

Pit Boy to Prime Minister

The story of
the Rt. Hon. Sir Joseph Cook, P.C., G.C.M.G.

G. Bebbington

To Keith
Best wishes,
Graham
Bebbington

Staffordshire Heritage Series
Editor J.H.Y.Briggs

Volume I

Centre of Local & Community History
UNIVERSITY OF KEELE, STAFFORDSHIRE
ST5 5BG

In loving memory of
my dear parents
Sydney & Alice E.Bebbington

ISSN 0950-7345

This publication has been generously sponsored by
Newcastle Borough Council and received financial
support from the Newcastle-under-Lyme Barracks Trust.

Printed in the UK by 4edge Limited

Contents

I Sir Joseph Cook, Detail from a painting by Guthrie.

Foreword

My fascination with local history stems back to my childhood at Silverdale when certain events were related to me by various people including my late parents, my grandmother and, of course, schoolteachers. Presumably had I not been interested in their recollections then I would not have listened so intently.

The name of Sir Joseph Cook was recalled on occasions and the story of how, having started to work at a local colliery at a very early age, he eventually emigrated to Australia to become, amongst other things, Prime Minister of that country. It was not until some years later that I decided to undertake research of his life having found that there was little information available locally, particularly regarding his early years.

This paper is the result of that research. Although of necessity politics are mentioned this is not intended to be a political biography. No attempt is made to justify the man's politics nor his apparent changes in political allegiance. This is simply an attempt to tell the story of his incredible rise to fame, something which appears to have been sadly lacking on the bookshelves.

The research for this paper has not been the easiest of tasks and certainly not aided by the necessity of having to communicate 'across the miles' to Australia on so many aspects. Research was made even more difficult by reason of Cook having, shortly before his death, destroyed his personal papers. I have, however, attempted to bring together published and unpublished material, official and unofficial, to tell his story. Whilst his personal papers were destroyed, relatives fortunately collected press cuttings and other mementoes such as invitations etc. and these treasured items have been made available to me and greatly assisted in the research.

To my knowledge, only J.R.M.Murdoch, in a PhD thesis, has attempted to relate Cook's political biography and I have drawn on this excellent work.

The greatest pleasure in writing this biography has been the kindness and courtesy I have encountered during my quest for information. This work would have been much the poorer and have taken much longer to produce but for the help of those who had memories to share with me.

To the many people who willingly afforded my wife

and I not only of their valuable time and the benefit of their experience but also hospitality, I am especially grateful. Those persons' names are appended overleaf and the writer apologizes if anyone has been omitted. I would also like to thank John Briggs, Paul Bemrose, Professor Frank Crowley and Dr.Brian Nixon for their invaluable comments and criticism. Also thanks to my dear wife Lynne Margaret who assisted with everything from tracing relatives to proof reading.

Finally, I think it incumbent upon me whilst extending thanks for all the help received to exonerate all others from any responsibility for this work's shortcomings. The responsibility is mine alone.

GB

Acknowledgements

The writer is greatly indebted to the assistance of the following:-

1) Great Britain

Relatives

The late Mrs.R.F.Cook MBE, BEM
Mrs.J.Fearnley
Mr.& Mrs.J.Hayward
Commander M.Hayward RN (Rtd) & Mrs.Hayward
Mrs.D.Holroyde
J.Riley

Also to the following:

D.Ainsworth, Press Officer, British Telecom
J.C.Andrews, Chief Librarian, Ministry of Defence
The late Arthur Bebbington
Harold Brown
Miss A.M.Colquhuon, Librarian, Australian High
Commission, London
Ann England ALA, Principal Area Librarian,
Newcastle-under-Lyme and her staff, in
particular:-
    Dave Adams (Area Reference Librarian)
    Jean White (who also helped with research in
    Australia)
Miss E.Evans, Assistant, North Staffs. Polytechnic
Library
Mrs.E.R.Gardner, Cabinet Office, London
Lt.Col.B.J.Hanley, Curator, Staffs. Regiment
Museum
Mrs.J.Hood, Information Officer, Lloyds of London
George Jebb, former Training Officer, Silverdale
Colliery
Miss G.Jones, Deputy Archives Officer, BBC
J.H.Kelly, Keeper of Social History,
Stoke-on-Trent City Museum
Mrs.D.Kelsall
Richard & Eileen Mills
Dr.W.Brian Nixon, B.A. Ph.D.
Stewart Oliver - Public Relations Department,
National Coal Board
D.Smith, Headmaster, Silverdale County Primary
School
J.Storm, former Headmaster, St.Lukes School,
Silverdale
The Editor & staff, Staffordshire Sentinel
newspapers in particular, Barbara Mansfield,
Librarian

G.Thompson, Guildhall Librarian, London
Mrs.K.M.Weaver
Arthur Wood, BBC Radio Stoke-on-Trent

and also the following colleagues at Newcastle
Borough Council:-

Paul J.Bemrose MA, FSA, AILAM, Curator
A.Clayton Davenport F.Inst.L.Ex. former Chief
Clerk & Members Information Officer
Liz Dodd - who translated my somewhat indifferent
handwriting
Joyce Doyle - secretarial assistance
John Grindey - art work (John and his wife Di also
kindly assisted with research in Australia)
Lynn Vodrey - Printing Supervisor

2) <u>Australia</u>

   <u>Relatives</u>   Mrs.M.Wood

   <u>Also to the following:</u>

   Rev.E.G.Clancy, Librarian & Archivist, Uniting
   Church in Australia (NSW Synod)
   Prof.Frank Crowley, University of New South Wales
   The Mitchell Librarian, State Library of NSW
   La Trobe Librarian, State Library of Victoria
   Prof.John N.Molony, Australian National University
   Geoffrey Sawer
   The Editor, Sydney Morning Herald
   The Principal Archivist & Staff, Archives Office
   of New South Wales.

3) Permission to reproduce the following items is
   gratefully acknowledged:-

I	National Gallery of Scotland
II	F.J.Rogers
III	P.J.Bemrose
IV & VII	D.B.Morris
V	H.Brown
VI & XIV	Newcastle-under-Lyme Library
X, XII & XIII	Mitchell Library, State Library of New South Wales
XIX, XXII & XXVII	Mrs.J.Fearnley
XXI	Mrs.D.Holroyde
XV, XVI, XXIV, XXVI & XXVIII	Mrs.M.Wood
XXV	E.Wetherell, Secretary, Newcastle Borough Council

   Every effort has been made to trace sources of
   photographs. The author apologises for any
   inadvertent omissions.

I Staffordshire Origins

- Introduction -

A Daleian is a person born at Silverdale, a mining village nestling in a valley in Staffordshire, approximately 2 miles west of the market town of Newcastle-under-Lyme. With the pleasant green hills and fields on either side, together with the woods of Keele, tucked in its valley Silverdale, prior to recent redevelopment, had the air of a Welsh mining village.

In the mid 19th century the village sprang up as a result of the growth of mines and ironworks in the area. It was, to quote my former schoolteachers, 'a child of the new industrial age'. In 1851 the population was a mere 2,000 but by 1861 this had more than doubled to 4,464, being entirely due to the exploitation of mineral resources in the area[1]. In fact a newspaper correspondent at the time wrote 'development is largely due to the efforts of Mr.Stanier of the Silverdale Company, whose extensive mills and forges are gradually converting a beautiful valley, worthy the name of Silverdale, into the smoke beclouded chaos which an iron making district presents'[2]. The rapid growth of the ironworks must have made any site near to the furnaces most unattractive and it is significant to note that the village tended to develop towards the south and east away from the mines and furnaces[3]. The village lay partly within the Parish of Keele and that of Wolstanton. However, as a result of the growth in population Silverdale was created a Parish in its own right by an Order in Council signed by Her Majesty Queen Victoria at Windsor on 21st November, 1855[4].

Most of the early workers' houses were built by Francis Stanier together with Ralph Sneyd of nearby Keele Hall. Both men patronised the village in their lifetime[5], Stanier leasing the Silverdale mines and furnaces from the Sneyds. At this time Silverdale families had a tendency to be large. Lighting in the houses was by candles or 'farthing dip', a primitive form of oil lamp. Heating and cooking was by means of a range with a large grate and tray oven, a cauldron or kettle being suspended over the fire. Clogs were worn to work and children often went barefoot[6].

Escape from the overcrowded conditions for the men was to the public house or walks into the lovely surrounding countryside and for the children to the streets. Some walks in the directions of Keele, Leycett, or Alsagers Bank afforded the most magnificent views of the Cheshire Plain and these, in particular, were popular with the miners as it enabled them to inhale the clean air carried across the plain from the sea. The view of the plain from Scot Hay Road was breathtaking and the Welsh mountains could also be seen on an exceptionally clear day.

The womenfolk, when not seeing to the needs of their family, strove to keep their homes clean which must have seemed to be an endless task. Generally the houses resembled little palaces inside but outside the cills and pavements were washed down daily in an effort to combat the dirt in the atmosphere which emanated from the chimneys of the mines and furnaces, etc. For those who were interested there were the occasional social activities such as bazaars, concerts, dances, etc. organised in the main by the church or chapel but these were infrequent. At that particular time, it is difficult to imagine a more unlikely place for a person to be born who was destined to become a Prime Minister. Nevertheless, such a man was born at Silverdale in 1860.

Generally, the period was an important one in the country's history. Queen Victoria had reigned for over two decades and Gladstone was Chancellor of the Exchequer. The industrial revolution was well in progress which meant that agriculture was now the static partner in the nation's economy although still wielding much of the nation's political power. Darwin's Origin of Species had not long been published and Livingstone was exploring the African continent having already discovered the Victoria Falls. The steamroller had been invented and the SS Great Eastern, the largest ship of her time (27,000 tons) had been launched. It was, without doubt, the beginning of a new era.

1.   Childhood

Joseph Cooke, born on 7th December, 1860[7], was the first son and second child of William and Margaret Cooke, the couple already having a daughter by the name of Sarah. She unfortunately died before she was 7 years old[8]. William and Margaret Cooke originated from Cheshire, he from Coppenhall, she from Knutsford[9]. They presumably came into the area seeking employment like so many other families at this particular time.

According to his birth certificate Joseph was born in Vale Pleasant, Silverdale, but by the time he was 3 months old the family were living in Brookside, another street nearby[10]. Brookside was a small cobbled street consisting of thatched properties with one room upstairs and one room downstairs. A back kitchen or wash house was detached from the property at the rear, this building also containing a privy. Some properties had gardens bordered by a brook which ran brown with waste water from the collieries. Rats, living in the bank of the brook, were a constant problem[11].

By 1871 Margaret Cooke had given birth to another four children, Sally (otherwise known as Sarah in memory of her deceased sister), Caroline, William and Albert and the family had moved to what is now 86 Newcastle Street[12]. Yet another child Emily, was to be born there in 1872[13].

The house in Newcastle Street, a terraced property, was situated at the eastern end of the village further away from the mines. It was a larger, pleasanter house than their former residence having open fields to the rear, although adjacent to a railway line.

Joseph's father, William Cooke, was a butty miner and was employed at the Silverdale Company's Hollywood Pit, one of a number of collieries nearby. A butty collier was a master of men: leasing a coal face from the management, he was responsible for its economic exploitation. He hired and fired men as necessary. Working conditions in the mines generally at this time were almost impossible. It was a nightmare world of darkness and despair and back-breaking labour. Men worked in constant danger. Tragedies were frequent and an important contributory factor was 'the prevalence of the subcontract or butty system of labour organisation. This system which put managerial power into the hands of men whose sole concern was maximum output at minimum cost, could only make more hazardous the lives of miners already faced with formidable dangers'[14]. Haste was an essential adjunct to the butty system and death and danger were its inevitable concomitants.

Where such a system was in operation the workmen were the servants of the butty and not of the colliery owner or proprietor. The butty contracted to deliver coal at a certain cost per ton and supplied his men with the necessary tools and equipment. One person recalled that in his younger days he overheard a butty addressing a young lad early one morning with the words "every ounce of flesh, every spot of blood, every drop of sweat of yours is mine today!"[15]. One can imagine the reaction that the miners, or any other worker, would have today if such attitude was adopted by management! It would be naive however to assume that all buttys had such an attitude towards their men but the emphasis was certainly on maximising production.

It is very difficult to generalise about wage rates. Competition for buttyships was keen and the buttys' margin of profit frequently narrow[16]. However, at this period the labourers they employed received approximately £2 per week[17] and juvenile labourers approximately 9d per day, or 1/- if they were fortunate[18].

As William Cooke was a butty collier his family's living standards would have been higher than those of an ordinary miner. He worked hard and, generally speaking, his industry ensured that his children lacked none of what, at present, would be considered to be basic necessities, whilst at the same time could not be regarded as in any way being 'pampered'[19]. Times were hard and the family did not by any means enjoy a life of luxury.

William and Margaret Cooke were happily married and they were extremely fond of their children. Margaret Cooke was of a sweet and charitable nature, very dignified, whereas William was a typical Victorian parent, being the disciplinarian of the family. He held the opinion that to spare the rod was to spoil the child. Strict discipline was the order of the day and punishment administered as necessary. William and Margaret were good parents, loving and fair and respected by their children and associates[20].

Joseph's school days were spent at St.Luke's Church of England School which adjoined the parish church. The headmaster was Mr.Edwin Smithyman, who according to an Inspector's report, was 'a painstaking master'[21]. Parents were expected to contribute a small amount towards the expenses incurred in educating their children at the school. However, this was beyond the means of some families. Later in 1872 when the Primitive Methodists opened a day school in High Street there was a tendency for some pupils to be transferred there as fees were often lower. Parents often ran up a debt for unpaid fees at one school then transferred their children to the other establishment sometimes following the same practice there.

St.Luke's school was a single storey building, boys and girls departments being separated by a folding partition. However the sexes were not allowed to mix during school hours. They were taught separately and had their own playgrounds. The school plans actually show the playground divided by what is described as an 'unclimbable' fence! Boys and girls even entered the school via separate entrances clearly labelled as such. Only in the infants department were boys and girls allowed to have lessons in the same classroom and use the same playground[22]. The classrooms had extremely high ceilings with large elevated windows so that children were not tempted to look out of them. Consequently the rooms were lofty and difficult to heat. Heating was by coal fired stoves which, according to the school log book, constantly smoked. A great deal of inconvenience was caused in the classroom as a result of great clouds of soot and smoke being emitted. There are also references in the school log books to the classrooms being too dark to work during afternoons.

Common colds, coughs and sore throats which were encouraged by the conditions in the school also kept large numbers of children away especially in the winter period. Inclement weather, particularly snow, usually resulted in a reduction in attendance. This was caused on occasion by children being soaked on going home at lunch time having no dry clothes or shoes to change into to enable them to return to school for the afternoon session[23].

At this period some of the children, particularly girls, attended the school on a part-time basis as factory scholars working in local textile factories for the remainder of the time. Smithyman taught some of these pupils, and others who had to leave school at an early age to seek employment, in the evenings to ensure that they were not disadvantaged through lack of education. These classes must have been some of the earliest examples of 'night schools' in the area[24].

Edwin Smithyman appears to have been an excellent headmaster and there are several references to his credit in the school log books. Not only was he painstaking in his work, but one Inspector also commented that 'discipline in the school deserves praise when the number of pupils is taken into consideration'[25]. In fact the school was grossly overcrowded, being the only one serving the village at the time.

Smithyman also received much assistance in the running of the school from the Vicar, the Revd. George Armitage, B.A., first incumbent of the Parish and a former curate of St.George's, Newcastle-under-Lyme. He came to the village when the Church of St.Luke was consecrated on 28th October, 1853[26]. There are frequent references in the log books to either the Vicar or his wife attending the school to take charge of a class. Revd. Armitage was much loved in the village and it is interesting to note that even to the day, Pepper Street where the old vicarage stood (now this replaced by a modern one) is still known by some residents as Armitage's Bank.

William and Margaret Cooke gave whatever help and encouragement they could to their children in relation to their school work. Possibly believing in the adage 'work is the rent that you pay for your life', they continually impressed upon them that success was

5

achieved by hard work and only came to those who were deserving of it. As with most large families at this time, Joseph and his brothers and sisters were trained to assist with household duties such as scrubbing floors, cleaning windows, polishing furniture and the preparation of meals. The Cooke children ran errands, not only for their own family, but for neighbours. Joseph too ran errands and also cleaned steps for neighbours for which he no doubt received a small recompense[27].

At the age of 9 years Joseph commenced working at one of the village collieries[28]. His duties included pushing and pulling wagons of coal (also known as tubs), attending to pit ponies, and oiling or greasing, which was normal for any pit boy at that time[29]. However, this was only to be for a brief period.

As a result of the Elementary Education Act, 1870 Joseph was "compelled to return" to his desk at the village school[30]. The Act, introduced by W.E.Forster, paved the way for elected school boards to be set up where that was desired, especially in urban areas where there was a shortage of school capacity. The Boards were empowered to raise money from the rates to finance themselves. The new legislation came as a result of Gladstone's Government and the people having recognised that the task of educating the great mass of children, the offsprings of the labouring and manufacturing poor, was beyond the means of voluntary resources alone. The enactment of compulsory education from the age of five to thirteen years was left to local decision, and its enforcement to local by-laws. Locally, however, an early attempt by the board to establish thirteen as the school leaving age met with protests from the owners of the Silverdale silk mill on the ground that they would lose a third of their labour force[31].

His short experience in the local coal mine taught Joseph to appreciate the value of what he had been missing in school and aided by Edwin Smithyman, his headmaster and his staff, the young man's intellectual activity was quickly stimulated[32]. At the age of twelve Joseph left school a second time and returned to his former employment at the local colliery. However, as a result of Smithyman's attention, together with that of his parents, an exceptionally strong ambition to improve his position became implanted in him. This ambition was to become one of his most prominent characteristics, revealed first in a drive for self-improvement and, later on in life, his determination to succeed in politics. However, it is also fair to say that help and encouragement was also given to Joseph's younger brothers and sisters all of whom were gifted in their own particular ways. Those who survived all went on to have successful careers[33].

2.   Tragedy

Joseph returned to work at the colliery where he had been previously employed. This was No.6 pit, otherwise known locally as 'Big Pit'[34]. The colliery was leased to Francis Stanier who at this particular period controlled all the Silverdale mines from which he supplied his ironworks with coal and ore, exporting a surplus of both[35]. Stanier served as Mayor of Newcastle-under-Lyme on three occasions and resided at Peplow Hall, near Market Drayton. He was a Deputy Lieutenant for Shropshire and also a Director of the North Staffordshire Railway Company[36]. At one time he was the largest employer in North Staffordshire controlling all branches of the ironworking industry from raw materials to foundry products[37].

No.6 pit was situated on the north side of Scot Hay Road approximately one mile west of Silverdale[38]. There was no proper highway at this time and one can imagine the condition the men and boys would have been in having trudged this length of road in inclement weather. Otherwise the walk would have been rather pleasant in the better weather, particularly in Spring, when the north side of the track became a profusion of yellow from pussy willows. There was also an abundance of silver birch from which the name of the village was said to have originated. According to an early historian, the whole of the valley had originally been covered with silver birch which, in the sunshine, resembled a 'dale of silver'[39]. Apart from a few cottages, Albert Terrace (otherwise known as the 'Treacle Row'), the other side of the road was bounded by fields and the large grounds of Silverdale House. The latter was the residence of Mr.T.Udall, an official of Stanier's company.

The headgear and buildings of No.6 pit stood out against the skyline on a prominent ridge of a hill. The mine ventilation was by means of a large waddle fan which drew air down the shaft. The deep throb of its revving could be heard in the village when the wind was in the right direction[40]. Conditions at the pit were particularly bad. Although there were flat areas where ponies were used, there were also some long steep gradients. There was a hot atmosphere and a high incidence of gob fires. Miners working there referred to it as the "Hell 'ole"[41]. Any young miner complaining about working conditions at nearby Kent's Lane colliery would be likely to receive a retort in broad North Staffordshire dialect - "Stop thaiy complainin' - thaiy wants a wick or two at th' owd No.6. That would put thaiy raight for this cushy 'ole here. Whey mining dine this pit is nearly flat and cowd compared with that bloody 'ole up thee-er!"[42]. On pay days the men from the pit sat at the roadside waiting to receive their wages from the butty. Frequently there were disagreements at such times which often resulted in fighting and then 'blood flew'[43].

In 1873 tragedy struck the Cooke family. On 8th April at 7.30 a.m. Joseph's father, William, was fatally injured in a mining accident. According to the Potteries Examiner under the heading of 'Awful Death' the report states that "he was said to be repairing rails in the dip when a full wagon coming down, came upon him with such force as to bring it to a standstill and tore up some of the rails. The wagon was at once spiked back off him but the poor man was only supposed to have spoken once, death being instantaneous. The brakesman is said not to have known that he was there in the dark"[44]. The Coroner, Mr.J.Booth, held an inquest at the Sneyd Arms, Silverdale and recorded a verdict of 'Accidental Death'. William Cooke was 39 years old[45]. Tragedy was to strike the family yet again some years later when Joseph's brother Albert aged 21 was killed at the local Sherriff Colliery. He was engaged on duties at the foot of the 500ft. shaft when a piece of coal fell down the shaft hitting him on the head[46].

It was common practice in mining areas, if a miner was fatally injured, for the whole shift to cease operations and walk behind the deceased's body until it was laid in his front room. There is no evidence to suggest that this did not happen in the case of William Cooke, particularly with him being the butty. Miners are a proud people. Although poor in life miners were lavish at funerals. A decent burial was considered to be of great importance. Everything had to be seen to be done correctly. Again, there is no evidence of the type of funeral which William Cooke had but he did have an excellent gravestone which, in those days, must have cost the family an appreciable amount.

The gravestone of William Cooke (and that of his children Sarah and Albert) may still be seen at St.Luke's churchyard, Silverdale[47]. It has stood defiantly against all weathers, the lettering still being quite legible despite a slight covering of moss.

William's inscription reads:

"Blessed are the dead which die in the Lord
            for they rest from their labours"

Most apt some would say in the circumstances. Sadly though such was the lot of mining families at this time as many of them could testify.

It is interesting to note that, at the time, H.M. Inspector of Mines Mr.T.Wynne commented that "the haste with which all underground work is now done has a tendency to make those young persons who are employed on inclines and on main roads think more of getting their work done in the limited time allowed than of their own safety"[48]. Such comments again highlight the criticisms of the butty system but were of little consolation to the widows and children left behind.

Improvements were made in the mines locally as a result of the establishment in 1872 of the North Staffordshire Institute of Mining and Mechanical Engineers. Members quickly began to study local conditions and publish their findings. Here for the first time was a group of local experts committed to resolving the whole range of problems associated with mining, the most important of which was the prevention of accidents and disasters[49]. Improvements quickly followed in the fields of haulage, ventilation and propping devices[50]. Also in 1872 Gladstone's Liberal administration passed the Coal Mines Regulation Act, the effect of which was that mines had to be tested for safety daily by deputy overseers. Also Mines Inspectors were to be appointed. The Act was one of the most important items in the development of the complicated legislation which governs pit safety. Although the Act and the formation of the Institute did bring about improvements which, in turn, helped to reduce the number of fatalities and the amount of human suffering, this did not, regrettably, help William Cooke who died under such tragic circumstances leaving a widow and six children.

The situation was no better described, albeit years later, than in J.Rusby's poem 'The Price of Coal' -

"Though black I am and hidden away
For millions and millions of years,
I have my price and some must pay
In sweat and blood and tears .....

O God of mercy, will it ever be
That safety for the miner we shall see?
Will he be wholly free from dread,
Whilst down the mine to earn his bread?"

3. Methodism

When families were bereaved as a result of a mining accident, generally speaking, they faced great

hardship.   Large scale disasters were usually followed
by public appeals for donations to a disaster fund and
subsequently a committee would most likely be elected to
administer the fund and organise relief.   However, in
the case of the odd fatality, tragic though it may have
been, no appeals were launched to assist dependents.   It
is fair to say, however, that in certain instances
benefit concerts were arranged.   Friendly societies did
exist which made provision for widows and dependents but
few miners were members as they often could not afford
the weekly payments[51].

On the death of his father, Joseph, as eldest son,
became head of the family and its principal breadwinner.
This placed quite a responsibility on him and he had not
yet attained his 13th birthday.   However, by having to
look after his mother and younger brothers and sisters
he became accustomed to acting on behalf of others, and,
as a result, rapidly grew to manhood with a highly
developed sense of protective responsibility[52].

Although originally attending St.Luke's Church at
Silverdale[53], the Cooke family became associated with
Primitive Methodism, a faith which was widespread among
the local miners.   In the latter part of the 18th
century Methodism was suffering from fragmentation.   Two
new sects emerged these being the New Connexion of
Methodists in 1797, and the Primitive Methodists (or
Ranters or Clowsites as they were frequently called) who
emerged in the first decade of the 19th century as a
result of the 'camp' meetings held at Mow Cop, a
prominent hill village on the Staffordshire-Cheshire
border[54].   It was not, however, until 1811 that the
Primitive Methodists organised any regular plan to send
preachers out to different villages etc. or to promote
the building of chapels in which to hold their
services[55].   The new sects reduced the possibility of
clerical control generally giving the laymen the
opportunity to manage their own affairs with a result
that their denominations evolved a purely democratic
system of management that not only worked admirably but
spread throughout the industrial centres of the country
in a remarkably short time.   A favourite local author
commented that the North Staffordshire Methodists'
philosophy of life was 'based on a set of gritty maxims
in which plain living, and high thinking ran a close
second to waste not, want not!'[56].

Young Joseph took advantage of the aid which the
Primitive Methodist movement gave to the youth of the
working classes and borrowed books from the local High
Street chapel where he and the family worshipped.   In
his lunch breaks at the mine he used to sit alone by a
pit lamp so that he could continue his studies.
However, I understand that he was not regarded as aloof

by his colleagues for this practice, but admired for his efforts to advance himself[57]. He was also known to have chalked on pit tubs to improve his spelling, writing and arithmetic[58]. On arriving home he would continue to study in the evenings by candlelight often until the early hours of the morning[59].

Although working 10 or 12 hour shifts, sometimes rising at 4 o'clock in the morning,[60] he contrived to lay the foundation of the education he afterwards extended by experience and discriminating reading. Later on in life he would recall how he would spend his last few pence on a book, attributing his love of books to the fact that he originated from Dr.Johnson's county[61].

His studies were, in a way, his recreation. He had no interest in sport unlike most of his young colleagues who played football and other games. He did swim however, during the warmer weather in local pools and in the canal in the nearby Apedale valley. He also went skating there during the winter[62]. The valley, lying some 1½ miles to the north east of Silverdale, became a favourite recreation area of his. By constant study he became very proficient at simple mathematics and learned to read quickly, also teaching himself to write a good standard of English in a clear hand[63].

Joseph joined Mr.J.Shenton's Bible Class at the chapel[64] and began to take more of an interest in Methodism. His faith helped him through the crucial years of his youth and became a source of inner strength to him. He began to preach at the age of 16 but within a short time he joined the Mutual Improvement Society formed by the New Connexion Methodists[65] at their premises on the corner of Church Street and Chapel Street, Silverdale. He was later to become the society's secretary and someone who was to become a life long friend, Arthur Hassam, was appointed treasurer[66]. It was at the society and at the Liberal Club in High Street, Silverdale, which he joined at 18, that he acquired his debating skills, subsequently to become so important in his late political career. The Liberal Club was visited by many prominent speakers including Joseph Chamberlain whom Cooke managed to hear[67].

The society was run by Dr.J.Mellor, the New Connexion Superintendent Minister. Probably as a result of the friendship and influence of Dr.Mellor, Cooke eventually left the Primitive Methodists and became a preacher on the local New Connexion circuit which had its head chapel at Ebenezer, Newcastle-under-Lyme.

Dr.Mellor gave Cooke the opportunity to address larger congregations and also offered to send him to the

Methodist New Connexion College at Ranmoor, Sheffield, to enable him to receive training for the ministry[68]. However, due to family circumstances he felt unable to take advantage of this generous offer.

He became a popular lay preacher and, according to some, an eloquent speaker showing indications of being a studied and deep thinker, emphasising points where necessary with a clenched fist on the pulpit or into the palm of his other hand. He was quite impressive in the pulpit and his sermons elicited the closest attention of the congregations before whom he appeared[69]. Although of medium stature he gave the impression of being taller than he was[70]. His work in the mine had helped build his physique and he took great pride in his appearance having developed an excellent posture. He had good hands and a bright shining blue eye[71]. Eventually he grew a moustache and beard which he kept for the rest of his life. He nonetheless always retained a well groomed appearance keeping his beard and moustache neatly trimmed[72]. A gifted orator, and a man with a purpose, he commanded respect wherever he went to speak[73]. Methodism not only provided him with his earliest opportunities of public speaking but also became a most important influence on his character.

It was at about this period that Joseph Cooke decided to drop the 'e' from his surname. He thought it pretentious and for the rest of his life he retained the name Cook. There is no evidence, however, that this action was legalised[74].

He continued to work the lengthy shifts at the mine sometimes not seeing daylight except on Saturday afternoons and Sundays which became a blessed day to him[75]. With working the hours that he did to support his family and, at the same time, pursuing his own studies, one could perhaps say of Joseph Cook that he achieved nothing without effort, but the effort came as natural as breathing.

4.   The Leaving of Silverdale

The possibility of disaster and the general conditions in the pits, together with the vulnerability of the miners to the fluctuating world demand for coal, led to primitive forms of unionism. In the Potteries area until the establishment of the North Staffordshire Miners' Federation in 1869 this was, however, spasmodic. A lodge served the Silverdale mines and in his late teens Cook, being perhaps more literate than most of his colleagues, became involved in the trade union work of the local miners, using his clerical skills to assist with the secretarial business[76].

Troubled times however were to come for the Silverdale valley and its inhabitants in the early 1880s for reasons which the trade unions could do little about. There was a depressed market and Francis Stanier decided not to renew the lease of the Silverdale colleries and ironworks. The editor of the <u>Newcastle Guardian</u> at that time commented that "Stanier would continue to work those mines and ironworks at Apedale, having recently enlarged his rolling mills at Knutton. The Silverdale Collieries are to be carried on by another firm and trade prospects look encouraging"[77]. But the Silverdale side of Stanier's empire was, in fact, past its best. Stanier had already, in fact, moved his headquarters to nearby Apedale which had not at that time reached its peak output. The Silverdale mines and ironworks were eventually taken over by the Butterley Company of Alfreton, Derbyshire[78].

Another problem was that competition from outside sources led to wage reductions in the coal and iron industries not only at Silverdale but throughout the whole of North Staffordshire. On a number of occasions this led to long and bitter strikes particularly in 1883 and 1884[79] which brought many families close to the poverty line. They could hardly afford to feed their children let alone pay school fees, a factor which no doubt had a large influence on the workers having to concede defeat in the majority of strikes. Furthermore, in most cases the employers were unable to pay an increase in wages and the workers had to return to work or face starvation. The unions were not strong enough to fight such disputes nor had they sufficient funds to support their members in lengthy strikes. The situation in the area eventually caused many families to leave and seek more rewarding employment, some even emigrating.

In an effort to supplement their diets some miners turned to poaching. They were almost inevitably caught and subsequently brought before the local Magistrates. There are several instances reported in the <u>Newcastle Guardian</u> one of which refers to two miners having been caught poaching pheasant in a hay field at Silverdale being fined 10 shillings each[80]. Such a fine represents an appreciable amount and illustrates how desperate some of the families had become.

Cook found himself in the position of trying to find alternative employment and eventually obtained temporary work with the North Staffordshire Railway Company (later to become affectionately known as the 'Knotty', from the Staffordshire Knot incorporated in its official emblem) cleaning and maintaining the engines at Whieldon Grove, Fenton[81]. This was the motive power depot of the company not only consisting of the normal engine sheds but also including a 'monster engine stable' or 'roundhouse' where Cook was employed. The 'roundhouse' was circular in form and approximately 200 feet in diameter. Besides general maintenance work, goods and carriages were manufactured there[82].

By this time Cook had also turned his attention to the gentler sex, having met a young lady by the name of Mary Turner. No one appears to know precisely how they met but it is assumed that they did so initially at a church function[83], possibly when Cook was a visiting preacher and introduced by a friend.

Mary was one of seven children of George and Ann Turner of Chesterton[84], another mining village approximately 2 miles to the north of Silverdale. The Turners were highly respected, the father being a coke burner by trade[85]. Mary was an Assistant Mistress at the Chesterton Girls' Board School in Albert Street, Chesterton. There is a reference to her credit in an Inspector's report quoted in the school log book to the effect that "her class had attained 96% although so backward when she took charge"[86]. (The percentage rate presumably refers to some scholastic achievement such as an examination).

Mary assisted and encouraged Cook with his studies and he became a regular visitor to the Turner household in Emberton Street[87] crossing the fields to Chesterton from behind his home at Silverdale[88] as often as time allowed. During their courtship the couple also frequently went walking along the canalside in the Apedale valley[89].

They were eventually married at the Primitive Methodist Church in London Road, Chesterton on 8th August, 1885, the ceremony being conducted by the Revd.J.Griffin[90]. The couple when considering their future came to the conclusion that prospects were brighter in the Colonies and decided to emigrate. It is perhaps fair to say that prior to this time Silverdale may have been the limit of Cook's horizon although he was keen to advance himself. However, Mary had a brother William who had already emigrated to Australia and was employed on the railways at Lithgow, New South Wales[91]. William's letters home to his family spoke highly of the employment prospects, regular wages – not to mention the equitable climate. Lithgow was not unlike Silverdale in size and it is possible that this was an added attraction to Cook. Furthermore 'having brought up one family under very hard conditions' Cook did not fancy the prospect of 'rearing his own children in like manner'[92] so they decided to emigrate to Australia and settle in Lithgow.

On 14th December, 1885 the local preachers of the

Newcastle circuit of the Methodist New Connexion met at Ebenezer, Newcastle-under-Lyme to pay their respects to Cook and to say farewell to their colleague. According to the <u>Newcastle Guardian</u> "after tea the Rev.J.Mellor presented Mr.Cook in appropriate terms with a revised edition of the Bible, Dilke's <u>Greater Britain</u>, the <u>Life and Epistles of St.Paul</u> and <u>Lord Tennyson's works</u>."

The works bore the inscription:

"Presented to Bro.Joseph Cook by the members of the Local Preachers Meeting of the Methodist New Connexion, Newcastle circuit on the occasion of his going to Australia expressive of their esteem for him as a Christian and fellow worker and the prayer that the Great Father may continue to care for him and his and make him in his new home, even than in his old home, a blessing to many[93]."

Between them the newly married couple had decided that, in view of their financial position, Joseph should proceed to Australia first in order that he could obtain work and prepare a home for Mary. In any case Mary by this time was pregnant.

December 1885 brought intense frosts making the roads and footpaths very dangerous[94]. The time of year and the situation locally caused the editor of the <u>Newcastle Guardian</u> to comment –

"the coal and minestone miners of Silverdale district have not acted upon their notice to cease work if a 10% in wages were not conceded. Apart from the merits of the case it would have been a misfortune for such work as can be obtained to stop now that the winter is with us and Christmas near at hand, for stoppage of work means stoppage of money[95]."

Cook, however, was to put all this behind him and on 25th December, 1885 he sailed in thick fog from Plymouth on the Pacific Steam Navigation Company's RMS 'John Elder' bound for Sydney[96] to prepare the way for his wife and future child.

Notes

1   <u>Keate's Gazetteer and Directory of Staffordshire</u> 1875

2   <u>Mining Journal</u> 10th May 1856

3   W.B.Nixon 'Iron industry of the Apedale and Silverdale Valleys of North Staffordshire 1768 - 1901.' Cambridge University BA Dissertation 1961. p.20

4   <u>Silverdale Parish Church Parochial Record Official Handbook and Souvenir of the Grand New Century Bazaar</u> 1901. p.55

5   W.B.Nixon <u>op.cit.</u> p.20

6   Anon. <u>The Parish of St.Luke, Silverdale</u> 1953. p.6

7   Birth certificate (Wolstanton Registration District)

8   Gravestone, St.Luke's Parish Church, Silverdale (Sarah died aged 6 years 10 months)

9   1861 population census

10   <u>Ibid.</u> In the thesis by J.Murdoch (NSW 1968) Cook is described as having been born at 86 Newcastle Street, Silverdale but the birth certificate states otherwise

11   Ex. info. H.Brown

12   1871 population census. Property identified by J.Haywood

13   Mrs.D.Holroyde (daughter of Emily). The excellent thesis by J.Murdoch unfortunately omits to mention Emily and also contains incorrect names of other sisters

14   A.J.Taylor. 'Coal' in <u>A History of the County of Stafford</u>. Vol II ed. M.W.Greenslade & J.G.Jenkins 1967. p.94

15   Ex. info. J.Haywood

16   A.J.Taylor. <u>op.cit.</u> p.100

17   Ex. info. H.Brown

18   A.J.Taylor <u>op.cit.</u> p.104

19   Ex. info. Mrs.D.Holroyde

20   Ex. info. Mrs.D.Holroyde and Mrs.M.Wood

21   Entry in school log book, 31st March, 1870

22   J.Ravenscroft 'State, School and Society - The Educational Environment of Silverdale and Chesterton 1862 - 1922'. University of Keele BA Dissertation 1974. p.5

23   Ibid p.40

24   There are several references in the school log book to evening classes including the entry of 2nd November, 1867 which refers to examination results for such classes

25   Entry in school log book, 18th March, 1871

26   Silverdale Parish Church Parochial Record Official Handbook and Souvenir of the Grand New Century Bazaar 1901. p.55

27   Ex. info. H.L.Whittaker. See also memories of old Silverdale - Newcastle Advertiser 11th February, 1983

28   Mrs.C.Bright - 'The Hon. Joseph Cook' in Cosmos Magazine, 31st March, 1896. p.269

29   Ex. info. H.Brown and G.Jebb

30   Cumberland Argus and Fruitgrowers' Advocate, 8th February, 1913

        (* These are Cook's words to a reporter but are questionable as the Act contained no provision which would have compelled him or others to return to school. It is just possible that economic reasons forced his parents to remove him from school to work at the mine and then the situation improved. This state of affairs was not unknown in the valley).

31   M.J.Cruikshank 'Spare the rod' in Newcastle-under-Lyme 1173 - 1973 ed. J.H.Y.Briggs 1973. p.151

32   Cumberland Argus and Fruitgrowers' Advocate, 8th February, 1913

33   Ex. info. Mrs.D.Holroyde

34   Ex. info. H.Brown

35   W.B.Nixon op.cit. p.7

36   County of Stafford and many of its family records
     W.Pollard & Co.Exeter 1897. p.55

37   W.B.Nixon op.cit. p.7

38   Ex. info. H.Brown and G.Jebb

39   Silverdale Parish Church Parochial Record Official
     Handbook and Souvenir of the Grand New Century
     Bazaar. 1901 p.39

40   Ex. info. H.Brown

41   Ex. info. H.Brown and G.Jebb

42   Ex. info. H.Brown

43   Ex. info. H.Brown

44   Potteries Examiner 12 April, 1873

45   Gravestone, St.Luke's Church, Silverdale.
     The Report of Inspectors of Mines for the year
     ending 31st December, 1873 briefly mentions the
     accident and records William Cooke's age as 35.
     However, this is not so reliable as ages were not
     quoted in all cases of fatalities

46   Gravestone, St.Luke's Church, Silverdale records
     date of death as 1st October, 1884. Report of the
     accident in Newcastle Guardian 4th October, 1884

47   The gravestone is no longer situated over the
     family grave as a lawn cemetery has been created
     and all monuments relocated to the rear of the
     churchyard.   It is not easy to find as it is
     immediately behind a beech hedge along with other
     gravestones.

48   Report of Inspectors of Mines. 1873 - 1874. p.73

49   L.Howe 'Causes and consequences of pit disasters
     in the North Staffs. Coalfield 1866 - 1918.'
     University of Keele BA Dissertation 1979. p.64

50   P.J.Bemrose   "Mines   and   Mills"   in
     Newcastle-under-Lyme 1173 - 1973 ed. J.H.Y.Briggs
     1973. p.100

51   L.Howe op.cit. p.45

52   Mrs.C.Bright.   op.cit.   p.269 and ex. info.
     Mrs.D.Holroyde

53 Mesdames D.Kelsall and K.M.Weaver

54 J.Ward. History of the Borough of Stoke-on-Trent 1843 p.98

55 Ibid

56 P.Oakes. From Middle England. 1980. p.10

57 Ex. info. J.Haywood

58 Ex. info. I.Jones

59 Ex. info. J.Haywood

60 Cook speaking during debate on Coal Mines Regulation Bill. NSW Parliamentary Debates 12th September, 1894. p.386

61 M.H.Ellis. 'Joseph Cook' in The Bulletin, 10th November, 1962 p.20 (see also Sentinel 6th September, 1918)

62 Ex. info. Mrs.R.F.Cook and Mrs.J.Fearnley (see also Cook's speech in the Sentinel 4th October, 1918)

63 Ex. info. Mrs.D.Holroyde

64 Sentinel, 5th September, 1918

65 Cumberland Argus and Fruitgrowers' Advocate, 8th February, 1913

66 Newcastle Guardian 3rd January, 1885

67 Cumberland Argus and Fruitgrowers' Advocate 8th February, 1913

68 Ibid

69 Sentinel 21st June, 1913

70 Ex. info. Mrs.D.Holroyde

71 M.H.Ellis. op.cit. p.21 and ex. info. Mrs.M.Wood

72 Ex. info. Mrs.M.Wood

73 Ex. info. Mrs.D.Holroyde

74 Ex. info. Mrs.D.Holroyde

75 Mrs.C.Bright. op.cit. p.269

76   It is rumoured that he held the post of Secretary but I have been unable to substantiate this. Personally I consider that due to his age and lack of experience this is highly unlikely. There is also a tendency to confuse the man with a namesake who was highly active in lodge affairs some years later.

77   Newcastle Guardian 17th June, 1882

78   P.J.Bemrose "Mines and Mills" in Newcastle-under-Lyme 1173 - 1973 ed. J.H.Y.Briggs 1973. p.99

79   A.J.Taylor. op.cit. p.105

80   Newcastle Guardian 1st August, 1885

81   Sentinel, 16th September, 1918

82   "Stoke-on-Trent" in Victoria History of the County of Stafford. Ed. J.G.Jenkins Vol.8 1963. p.209

83   Ex. info. Mrs.D.Holroyde and J.Riley

84   Ex. info. J.Riley and 1881 population census

85   Marriage certificate of Joseph Cook and Mary Turner (Wolstanton Registration District)

86   Entry in school log book, 11th November, 1885

87   Ex. info. J.Riley

88   Sentinel, 16th September, 1918

89   Sentinel, 4th October, 1918

90   Marriage certificate of Joseph Cook and Mary Turner (Wolstanton Registration District). The Australian Dictionary of Biography incorrectly records the marriage as having taken place at Wolstanton Primitive Methodist Chapel

91   Mrs.C.Bright. op.cit. p.269 and Cumberland Argus and Fruitgrowers' Advocate, 8th February, 1913

92   Mrs.C.Bright. op.cit. p.269

93   Newcastle Guardian 19th December, 1885

94   Newcastle Guardian 12th December, 1885

95   Ibid

96   Sailing details - Lloyds list and passenger list - New South Wales Archives (Shipping Masters Office (AO ref. XI79, reel 471))

II   Sneyd Terrace, Silverdale, showing the still rural atmosphere of the mining village with better-off employees' housing, with bay windows and railed gardens.

III   The chapel that played a large part in Cook's early nurture, Bethel New Connexion Chapel, at the end of its life awaiting demolition in 1973. The New Connexion Methodists were particularly strong in North Staffordshire being partly born out of a crisis in the Hanley Circuit.

IV   St Luke's Church and schools with the Headmaster's House in the centre. Cook began his education at the school to the left of the picture.

Coal and Iron

V   Life in Silverdale focused on the several pits that offered employment. This picture shows the engine house and winding gear for the shaft at the Big Pit where Cook was employed as a pit boy.

VI   Trucks being wound up the shaft at the Big Pit with
representative workers of the pre-first world war period.

VII   Silverdale Furnace: much of the coal cut at Silverdale
was employed within the village in iron production until the
furnaces in the area began to close in the 1880s.

VIII & IX   Sir Joseph and Lady Mary Cook, after Cook had received his
knighthood in 1918. Mary Cook, from Chesterton, Staffordshire ably
supported her husband in all his public life, and as much as he,
flourished in the new world of Australia, in particular undertaking
distinguished work for the Red Cross.

II Established in Australia

1.   The Land of Opportunity

The 4150 ton RMS 'John Elder', with Cook among its passengers, arrived in Sydney on 12th February 1886[1]. The long sea voyage must have been a strange experience for Cook for it is most likely that he had never travelled far outside his native Staffordshire before[2]. It must have seemed even stranger, having left England in such freezing conditions, adjusting to Sydney's climate which, at the time, was extremely warm and sunny. In fact a historian visiting the city at that time commented particularly on the weather, noting that the Acting Premier of New South Wales, the Rt. Hon. W.R.Dalley was "busy making history in his shirtsleeves"[3]. After a short stay in Sydney Cook proceeded to Lithgow to seek employment.

Lithgow is situated on the north western fringe of the Blue Mountains in New South Wales. It is just under 100 miles from Sydney and 3017ft. above sea level. Following an extension of the railway to the town in 1869 four coal mines were opened in the district and Lithgow, together with its adjacent settlements of Eskbank and the Vale of Clwydd, developed.

Industrial growth was rapid in the 1870s and it is interesting to note that Australia's first meat chilling works was built there in 1873. By 1880 there were also two copper smelting works, brickyards, tile works, a tannery and a brewery which used hops grown in the area with excellent results! In 1885 an ironworks, including a large blast furnace, began operation. In 1869 the population of Lithgow was a mere 100, but by 1885 it had exceeded 3,000.

Cook obtained work as a skilled miner at the Vale of Clwydd colliery[4] and in his spare time commenced building a house in Macauley Street. It was a detached property, constructed from timber, and he named it 'Silverdale' after his birth place in England[5]. Not for one moment forsaking his religious interests, he joined the Primitive Methodist Church at Lithgow soon after his arrival and became a local preacher[6].

With the little spare time that he had from house building and from his association with the church, Cook continued with his studies, particularly in the subjects of arithmetic, book-keeping and shorthand as he had a desire to become a journalist or an accountant. However it was not until some months later, January 1887, that he was able to take advantage of more serious study.

That month heralded the arrival in Australia of Cook's wife, Mary, and the son he had never seen. George Sydney Cook (later to become affectionately known by the family as 'GS'[7]) had been born at the home of Mary's parents in Emberton Street, Chesterton on 8th March 1886[8]. Having his wife and son now beside him Cook desired more than ever to advance himself. Mary, as a former schoolteacher, did all she could to encourage her husband in this respect and, at the same time, advised him how to acquire the necessary skills. Cook pursued his studies during any free moment. His wife, if not correcting his arithmetical efforts, would read aloud long passages from books as her husband struggled to master shorthand. Cook eventually won a prize, a dictionary, for his shorthand and became equally competent at book-keeping[9]. It is doubtful, however, if Cook realised how important shorthand would be to him later in life as he pursued his political career.

Cook did not neglect his reading and like many other aspiring working men became interested in the works of Ralph Waldo Emerson, the American essayist, poet and philosopher. Later in life he stated that he owed most of his mental development to Emerson, reading frequently his essays which continually inspired him[10]. Emerson decreed that 'men were exalted creatures, instinct is to be obeyed and that the soul is a sensible reality"[11]. Cook no doubt was also inspired by another of his mentor's utterances - "let men but stand erect and go alone and they can possess the universe!"[12]

In 1887 Cook was fortunate to realise one of his ambitions by obtaining a part-time managerial post with a local weekly newspaper, The Lithgow Enterprise and Australian Land Nationaliser[13]. Unfortunately, although successful initially, the newspaper ceased publication in January 1889 through lack of support from the local populace[14]. However by 1890, having acquired a good working knowledge of book-keeping, Cook was successful in gaining another part-time position, this time as auditor to the local Municipal Council[15].

Having been briefly associated with trade union affairs at his native Silverdale, Cook began to take an interest in lodge matters at the Vale of Clwyd colliery eventually holding the posts of president and secretary[16] respectively. Having listened as a boy to his father and, later, to the advice of older miners who had learned from bitter experiences, Cook had long come to the conclusion that strikes were not necessarily a satisfactory method of achieving improved working conditions. He had seen with his own eyes in England the starving families which had resulted from withdrawal of labour and the humiliation of the miners having returned to work after a lengthy strike with little or no concessions gained. Consequently, in any dispute he would attempt to reach agreement by negotiation and, at the same time, endeavour to restrain any 'brothers' who favoured a more militant approach. Needless to say, like most trade union officials, he was not always successful in this respect.

New South Wales had nothing to compare with the worst mining conditions in England but they were, nevertheless, bad enough. A correspondent of the Sydney Morning Herald visiting the coalfields in 1860, commented "To a stranger the exploration of a pit is not a very pleasurable occupation. Even where the mine is well ventilated the odour is necessarily offensive and unwholesome: the floor which is scarcely ever dry, renders it difficult to avoid getting feet wet; while the low roof often prevents your walking upright. In some pits the working is only 4ft. in depth and to examine them you must creep along in a stooping and uncomfortable posture"[17]. Seams of up to a thickness of 30ft. or more were worked in the colony. The very richness of the seams, whilst having obvious advantages, created difficulties if all or even a large part of the coal was to be won. Wide differences of opinion existed as to the best methods of working and this was reflected in the varying practices adopted in different mines[18].

In 1886 Cook was elected check-weighman at his colliery which was a most responsible position. Under the Coal Mines Regulation Act all coal mined had to be weighed at the mouth of the pit to enable pay to be assessed for each miner on the basis of an agreed sum per ton[19]. This was the responsibility of the check-weighman. He was appointed by the miners who also paid his wages and he generally looked after their interests[20].

On occasion Cook would air his views to the local press by submitting a letter for publication. This was particularly so when he felt the need to take the respective editor or a correspondent to task about an item which had been featured. An example is a letter which appeared in the Australian Star on 29th December 1887, (Illustration XI) a period when Cook was identified as a Protectionist. In this letter, Cook, demonstrating a continued familiarity with industrial development in his home country, passionately attacked the human consequences of free-trade, citing the example of the lay-offs caused in Staffordshire amongst the iron-workers because of the importation of cheap Belgian iron. Working short hours at low rates the men had become destitute and in practice (as against theory) were not free to seek employment elsewhere, even if available. It is doubtful if any of the readers of Cook's letter, unless they knew him personally, could ever have imagined his humble beginnings and that he was more or less self-educated, for the style of the letter does not reveal it. Whether readers agreed with the content is, of course, an entirely different matter.

On 9th July 1888 the Vale Colliery was officially opened at Lithgow followed by a banquet given by the mine directors for leading citizens at the Imperial Hotel. Cook was invited to propose a toast to the miners and in his address he stated that -

"he hoped the new company and their miners would be able to work together, for the time had gone by when capitalists could drive the laborers (sic) like the slave in bondage"[21].

Such aggressive style of speech, developed in the pulpit and at debating society meetings made him popular with the miners and, in January 1889, Cook was elected General Secretary of the Coal Miners Mutual Protective Association of the Western District (otherwise known as the Western Miners' Association) a post he held until 1891 when he entered politics[22]. The association had been formed in 1886 from all the mining unions in the Lithgow area and, as its representative at various conferences, Cook became one of the most respected trade unionists in New South Wales at that time. He was perhaps fortunate that his terms of office with the lodge and that of the association coincided with years in which the mining industry expanded, which aided his popularity. For example coal production in the colony in 1860 was 368,000 tons. In 1880 it was 1,466,000 tons and this had more than doubled by 1890[23].

The coal industry expanded as part of the general growth of the economy. The early development of the large cities, the extension of the railways and their conversion to coal burning, the establishment of coal gas as the normal means of public and private lighting in a society whose population almost trebled between 1860 and 1900 were the reasons for the expansion of demand[24].

2.   The State Legislative Assembly

In 1891 Cook was asked if he would be prepared to allow his name to be put forward as a Labor[25] candidate for Hartley in the forthcoming general election. Lithgow was situated in the Hartley constituency, which returned two representatives to the New South Wales Legislative Assembly at Sydney. After much persuasion, particularly from Mr.J.Ryan, the editor of the Lithgow Mercury[26], he allowed his name to be put forward only to be narrowly defeated in the selection by the

Revd.G.Smailes, a Primitive Methodist minister[27]. However Cook was not to be denied the nomination since, on account of illness, Smailes was obliged to withdraw· As a consequence Cook was invited and agreed to replace him. In the ensuing contest on 20th July Cook won one of the seats polling the highest number of votes, some 350 in advance of his nearest opponent[28].

In that campaign Cook learned how to conduct himself in an election and had his first lessons in political warfare. Among the other six candidates were two Free Traders, namely, John Hurley, a retiring member, and Francis Tabrett, a wealthy industrialist. Cook experienced some bitter attacks from these two opponents who both made disparaging remarks to the electorate to the effect that he would not represent Lithgow properly. In particular the former contended that Cook could not possibly know sufficient about conditions in New South Wales having only been in the country for a period of six years whilst the latter alleged that, if elected, Cook would only represent the miners[29]. Cook, however, came to appreciate that making venomous jibes at your opponent was part of the traditions of politics. At the nomination ceremony at Lithgow he retaliated saying -

> "My remarks will be in criticism of the various speakers seeing that they have had shots at me. If they had not interfered with me I would not have had anything to say about them ....."

He then went on to deliver blistering attacks against Tabrett's record as an employer and Hurley's financial record[30]. Some years later, it is obvious from an article he wrote for _Life_ magazine that he came to appreciate that the public liked to hear opponents criticising each other on a personal note[31].

Cook campaigned as a Labor candidate before there was a Labor party in Parliament so he had no experience of the need to keep to a rigid party line. His primary loyalties were to the people of Lithgow[32]. He wanted, amongst other things, female suffrage and better education facilities for poor children. By now he also supported land reform and notwithstanding his earlier protectionism was now a persuasive advocate of free trade. As a miner he stressed the need for improved working conditions and an eight hour day[33]. The eight hour working day movement had been active for some years in the colony, the stonemasons having gained the concession as far back as 1855. As the trade unions grew in Australia in the 1860s and 1870s a shorter working day was sought by the various skilled trades[34]. Wages were relatively high and the obvious means of improving the life of the working man was to reduce the length of the working day. For trade unionists the eight hour day was the pre-eminent symbol of achievement and a necessary condition for the moral and intellectual welfare of the working class. Coalminers were the first important group of workers outside the ranks of the skilled artisans to advocate a reduction in working hours[35].

Following his election the editor of Sydney's Daily Telegraph commented that the new Member "was essentially a moderate man and more likely to go in for steady progressive legislation than for any policy of violent reconstruction of society"[36]. For the first session Cook was scarcely heard in the House. He was busy learning the routine of parliamentary life from the opposition benches and making mental notes of his new surroundings[37]. As was his usual practice Cook took his new role very seriously. He could never commit himself to any task anything less than 100%[38]. It is perhaps that very serious disposition that lead some people to believe that he was humourless.

Cook found his shorthand ability of great use in his political career from the beginning but particularly so in later years. He made prolific notes in debates and confounded many an opponent by being able to quote, verbatim, the words that he, the opponent, had just uttered. Opponents generally came to appreciate that it was of little use denying having said something whilst up against Cook in a debate. By use of his shorthand notes his speeches became renowned for their correct wording and delivery[39]. He soon established himself as a competent parliamentary debater.

In 1893 Labor members polarized into Protectionist and Free-Trade sections and Cook was chosen unopposed as leader of the latter. Soon, however, there was a conflict of opinion between those of the party who upheld the principle of free radicalism and those who believed in the party pledge and the caucus machine. At a special conference of the Labor Electoral League in March 1894 a decision was taken which required every Labor member to pledge himself 'to vote in the House as a majority of the Party, sitting in caucus, has determined'[40]. Cook retorted that "the pledge destroys the representative character of a member and abrogates the electoral privileges of a constituency". William M.Hughes, a fiery protaganist of the measure responded that "the repression of the individual will involved does not concern us because no one is bound to come into the movement or forced to remain in it"[41]. The majority of Labor Members of the Legislative Assembly, including Cook, repudiated the pledge agreed to by the conference[42]. Cook withdrew to the ranks of the Labor independents, though as their leader he was foremost in bringing about some form of unity so that at the next election the Labor interest might not appear to the electorate too disunited[43].

Cook was never too busy to try to solve any problems of his constituents, but in a way this came naturally to him. Having developed an early sense of protective responsibility due to the tragic death of his father he had become accustomed to acting on behalf of others in his capacity as eldest son. Thus he developed a panache for dealing with people[44]. He served on various poor relief and charity committees and did all he could to find work for the constituency's unemployed. This particularly earned him widespread respect. The editor of the <u>Katoomba Times and Blue Mountaineer</u> commented that "by his past actions he has proved himself to be a man of great ability and what is more his ability is not abused. It would be a sin to keep such a man out of Parliament"[45].

At the next election on 17th July, 1894 Cook stood as an Independent Labor candidate retaining the Hartley seat with a good majority. George Houston Reid (later Sir) leader of the Free-Trade Party had been invited to form a Ministry following which he astonished Cook by offering him the Cabinet post of Postmaster General. This was seen as not only an attempt to anchor Cook and his followers to Reid's Free-Trade Party to facilitate a working majority, but also to placate Labor. Some also considered Cook's inclusion as a shrewd move by Reid to give his Cabinet a Labor tinge. Cook, however, approved of Reid's programme of reform legislation and following consultation with his supporters, he accepted the offer. He felt justified in doing this as he believed that he would be in a better position to serve not only Labor's interests but also those of his supporters and constituents, as a Minister than he would as a back bencher. He stated, in fact, that he accepted the post because "I saw my way to do so honourably and with justice to myself and those with whom I have been associated"[46].

However at that time new government ministers had to seek re-election before they could formally assume their duties. As a consequence Cook recontested his Hartley seat under the Free-Trade banner and was again returned with a large majority[47]. The Hartley constituents had once more shown that they had faith in Cook but to the pledged members of the Labor party his desertion was an act never to be forgiven. Henceforth, now being a Minister of the Crown, he was to be known as the Honourable Joseph Cook.

Reid was born in Johnstone, near Paisley, Scotland the son of a clergyman. He was portly with protruding sleepy looking blue eyes, and looked the embodiment of laziness and good humour. Any new political opponent taking him at facial appearance soon found themselves at a disadvantage. He possessed a rapier power of repartee that made him respected by political adversaries. Known to be an admirer of attractive women, Reid never took himself too seriously.

Cook was 33 years old when he became Postmaster General and he held the post for 4 years. Whilst he was in office he was determined to improve the efficiency of the postal service. One of the first tasks he undertook was a complete review of his department with a view to effecting retrenchment. Sydney's Daily Telegraph in 1895 reported that during the first three months of the year a sum equal to approx. £3,000 a year had been saved. This was achieved by redeployment of staff and retiring several sexagenarian officers some of whom had already attained retirement age some years before[48]. Cook was a firm believer in cheap telegraphic communications and authorised the construction of Australia's first long distance telephone connection between Sydney and Newcastle, and encouraged the development of a telephone network. In 1896 the same newspaper reported a boom in telephones because of Cook having reduced charges. The cost of a three minute telephone conversation was one shilling[49]. That same edition of the newspaper reported that, due to the boom, supplies of telephones had run out and that Cook, at that time, had more miles of telephone under his control than the Postmasters General of the whole of Australia and Tasmania. Cook effected another saving by employing young female labour in the telephone exchanges. They were paid on a scale of 10 shillings to 30 shillings per week according to 'capacity and ability'[50]. Cook also presided over the Postal and Telegraphic conference held at Sydney in 1896 which recommended extension of the Pacific cable to connect Vancouver with Australia[51].

Also in his capacity as Postmaster General, Cook expedited the installation of telegraphic lines underground as opposed to overhead, and likewise, the relaying of existing lines underground. He was of the opinion that overhead installations were not only 'a great eyesore but also a source of danger in case of fire'[52]. In taking this decision Cook had the foresight to realise, even at that time, how much overhead lines would detract from the amenities of towns, cities and the countryside. Cook was also the first Postmaster General to introduce charity stamps and use of bicycles into the postal service[53].

He was quite successful as Postmaster General. If any criticism can be levelled at him, as it invariably was, it is perhaps that he insisted on being involved in

28

even the most mundane matters and having full control. Nevertheless, it was largely due to his efforts that, during his term of office, New South Wales led Australia in progress made in postal services. Also during such period New South Wales was the only Australian colony to have balanced postal budgets[54].

In 1898 there was a Cabinet reshuffle and on 27th August Cook was appointed Secretary for Mines & Agriculture[55]. During the short period he held this portfolio he visited mining areas with a view to encouraging investment, also authorising mineral surveys to reveal the presence and extent of deposits. His keenness to promote the industry earned him praise from the mining reporter of Sydney's <u>Daily Telegraph</u> who commented that Cook "was a man of action who has already shown that he is amenable to reason, who is not prepared to follow the traditional do nothing usages of the department". The correspondent also praised "the promptitude with which Mr.Cook has dealt with several important matters which have been pigeon-holed in the department for months if not years ..... at last we have struck a Minister who represents "good pay-dirt!"[56]

From an agricultural aspect he was equally concerned to improve standards of production and appointed a scientist, William Farrer, as Government wheat experimentalist. He also arranged for lectures throughout the colony on new techniques varying from the prevention of tuberculosis to the extermination of pests in fruit.

Farrer's experiments were extremely successful and in 1924 Cook paid tribute to him in a book published to coincide with the British Empire Exhibition. Cook was the author of the section on Australia: of Farrer's work he wrote "the appearance of red rust had stopped wheat growing on many of the most fertile and best watered lands of the older states ..... Farrer bred wheats that would resist rust and other pests and so restored profitable wheat cultivation to many fields from which it had been absent. He improved the milling properties of the grain, reared stocks specially suitable for the interior and thus enlarged the scope and area of wheat cultivation very greatly, while at the same time diminishing its risks. Before he died he established varieties of wheat respectively suitable for the local conditions of any part of Australia where tillage is possible. He so improved the returns of grain that many millions were added to the income of the farmer"[57].

In 1899 the Reid government was defeated as a result of Labor giving its support to the Protectionists led by W.G.Lyne. During its period of office since 1894

Reid's administration had produced some of the most progressive legislation ever placed on the colony's statute book[58]. Cook had been quite successful in Cabinet, building up a reputation as an efficient administrator, completely loyal to Reid. In fact in his memoirs Reid commented that Cook was "a singularly able and devoted colleague"[59]. So Cook returned to the opposition benches no doubt taking consolation in the fact that he would be able to devote more time to his family and local affairs. By tradition, however, he retained the 'honourable' title.

By 1900 Joseph and Mary Cook had six children. In addition to George Sydney, born in England, there was Albert, Joseph William, John Hartley, Annette Margaret and Winifred Emmie[60]. The family were also living in a larger house in Bank Street, Lithgow having moved there in 1894[61]. Joseph and Mary were regarded as affectionate, strict, but loving parents[62], Joseph no doubt influenced by his own late father's attitudes and his up-bringing in Staffordshire. Cook regarded Mary as the best of good wives[63]. Temperamentally they were ideally suited and remained devoted to one another throughout their marriage. As Cook pursued his political career and became more successful he was continually absent from home for periods and his wife was responsible for bringing up the children and running the household but at the same time creating an atmosphere of rest and contentment where, on his return, he could quickly recover his energies. He came to like the occasional cigar and at home particularly if there were no guests, he loved to relax and drink his tea from a saucer[64]. A relative having witnessed this spectacle wondered, as a child, who on earth this special person was as he was not banished from the table! The Cook children regarded their father's return home as 'red letter days' and on Sunday evenings all the family would gather around the fireside where the children would tell stories or read favourite passages from books or sing hymns or popular songs of the time[65].

Cook also found time to correspond with relatives back home in England writing lengthy letters, a practise he maintained for the rest of his life. He also maintained his friendship with Arthur Hassam and John Shenton, his former Bible Teacher.

The Primitive Methodist Church at Lithgow was extremely active and Cook, in addition to lay preaching, became a Trustee of the Church. He often preached at anniversaries and at other Primitive Methodist Churches in New South Wales. Frequently on the Methodist platform, he became a prominent layman, probably the most prominent layman of the time and was a delegate to the Primitive Methodist Conference and a speaker at their public meetings[66]. Chairing the public meeting of the conference in 1894 he said that he was "pleased that the Churches were no longer afraid of socialism and that the clergy were dealing with social issues of the day"[67]. That same month he addressed members of the Annandale Church, Sydney on "The Brotherhood of Man"[68]. Cook was also a delegate to the Committee of various Methodist bodies which subsequently resulted in their amalgamation into one denomination. He again chaired the public meeting of the Primitive Methodist Conference in 1895 which was also celebrating the Jubilee of the founding of the Church in New South Wales. The subject of Methodist Union was then very much to the fore and Cook in addressing the conference said "one of the most pleasing features of the programme was the reception of the delegates of the Wesleyan body. As church people we ought to be capable of growing together just as was the case in other departments of life". To loud cheers he continued that he hoped that their centenary meeting would not be a meeting of Primitive Methodists, but of Methodists of New South Wales. He hoped that they would sink their very minor differences and get into closer association. He continued "The time has arrived when we should join hand in hand for the purpose of consolidating the forces of Christianity. I would not mind if we could clasp hands with more than our brother Wesleyans, if the next day we can clasp with the hand of friendship all who believe in Christianity and hope for its advancement"[69]. Following the Methodist Union in 1902 Cook continued to take a very active part in the Church[70].

Parliamentary business, however, continued to keep him occupied although in opposition, as there was much to interest him in Lyne's legislative programme including old age pensions, early closing of shops and mining reforms etc. Cook was successful in 1900 in persuading the Assembly to pass his Private Members Bill which sought to prevent wages being paid other than in money (that is he belatedly secured an Australian Truck Act)[71]. His successor as Secretary of Mines & Agriculture, J.L.Fegan, slightly modified some of Cook's earlier mining reform proposals and piloted them through the Assembly, so that even after he had left office, his influence was still being felt.

3.   Federation

In the 1890s many of the foundations of twentieth century Australia were laid no doubt due partly to the emergence of a federal movement. Although federation was a political matter it cut across all political parties of the time. Thus federalists consisted of Liberals,   Conservatives,   Protectionists,   and

Free-Traders etc. Following a series of referendums, particularly in 1899, on a draft constitution, the new century brought to a close the colonial chapter of Australia's history and the subsequent union of the six colonies (Victoria, Queensland, New South Wales, Tasmania, South Australia and Western Australia) into "one indissoluble Federal Commonwealth under the Crown of the United Kingdom". The legislation which brought about the union was the Commonwealth of Australia Act, a statute of the United Kingdom Parliament, which received the Royal Assent on 9th July 1900. This provided for, amongst other things, a combined responsible democratic parliamentary government on the lines of the British model (the system which had previously existed in the six colonies) with a federal distribution of powers between the Commonwealth and the six state (former colonial) governments on the general lines of the American constitution, the Commonwealth being entrusted with those matters which were national in character (e.g. defence, external affairs, banking and currency, immigration etc.) and the states retaining the undefined residue (e.g. railways, roads, health, education, industrial matters etc.)[72].

The Commonwealth of Australia came into existence on 1st January 1901 following a proclamation, made under warrant from Queen Victoria, by the first Governor-General, the Earl of Hopetoun, in Centennial Park, Sydney[73]. More than a hundred thousand people gathered in the park to watch the ceremony inaugurating Australia's first national government and to see Edmund Barton, a member of the New South Wales Legislature and acknowledged leader of the federal movement, sworn in as the country's first national Prime Minister[74].

Melbourne was chosen as the seat of government where it remained until being transferred to a new parliament house at Canberra in 1927.

The first elections for the Federal Parliament were held in March 1901. Standing as a Free-Trader, Cook contested the new Parramatta seat polling 5778 votes against his opponent, W.Sandford, a Protectionist and wealthy industrialist who gained 3646 votes[75]. The Parramatta seat included Lithgow and most of the Hartley State electorate and Cook was to hold it for 20 years. The electoral area was very diversified in that in addition to mining and other heavy industries there were rural activities such as fruit growing and market gardening. So Cook joined George Reid and his colleagues on the opposition benches of the newly assembled House of Representatives. A painter, Tom Roberts, who recorded such occasions on canvas noted that Cook was then 5' 9" in height, weighed 12 stone and had a hat size of 7![76]

As a consequence of his victory, and in order to be closer to both his new constituency and to party offices in Sydney, Cook and his family moved to a new home in Francis Street, Marrickville[77]. Marrickville was a middle-class area lying just north of Botany Bay and had the added advantage of being situated on the main railway line, thus making commuting to Melbourne easier for the Parliamentary sessions. When time allowed Cook would take his children swimming in the sea. He was of the firm opinion that, particularly in coastal areas, children should be taught swimming as part of the school curriculum[78]. As another form of relaxation Cook liked to fish but it is doubtful if he was ever so fond of this occasional preoccupation as he was of his beloved books. He regularly attended the little Methodist church at The Warren in the town and on occasions preached there[79].

The working of the first Federal Parliament was far from smooth. Although a new 'nation state' had been created, the members of the new legislature had no experience of working in a single national government, or loyalty to it, having only been acquainted with colonial government. Loyalty to former colony transcended loyalty to the new Federal Parliament and, therefore, parochialism was rampant[80]. Cook initially viewed all matters from a New South Wales aspect. For example when the question of the future federal capital was under debate he opposed Melbourne and spoke at length on the advantages of Bathurst which was the nearest of the proposed sites to his own constituency[81]. But he was not alone in this respect, most members following the same practice, the reasons being lack of experience of the new type of government and parochial selfishness. It was therefore some time before things really settled down.

Following the second federal elections in 1903 George Reid formed a coalition ministry with Allan McLean of the Protectionists. Although Cook was successfully returned to the House of Representatives, he was not offered a post in the Cabinet. The Reid-McLean Administration, however, was short-lived, lasting only until July 1905 as it never had a greater majority than two, and when the House sat as a Committee one of the two took the Chair![82] To describe the situation Reid in his momoirs wrote "To make bad worse, the one who was left was a supporter of the most doubtful kind. Coalitions at all times are full of elements of disaster but a coalition that was only half a coalition and had only one (when in Committee) a majority of one — who could not be depended upon — that surely was a situation not devoid of humour"![83]

In 1905 Cook became deputy leader of the

Free-Traders but after Reid's retirement in November 1908 he was elected leader. Reid had a very active legal practice at Sydney, being frequently absent and on such occasions Cook deputised for him. Reid acknowledged Cook's services in his memoirs stating "the able and devoted services of Mr.Joseph Cook, as deputy leader of the Opposition, were the main factors in making my position tolerable. Had he been less able, or less loyal, or less devoted than he was, a leadership so long and suspended as mine could not have lasted for a single session .... I therefore retired hoping that Mr.Cook would be chosen in my place. Mr.Cook was chosen as he richly deserved to be"[84]. On the occasion of his elevation to Leader of the Opposition, Henry Gyles Turner described Cook as a man "possessed of an incisive vigour in debate, a thorough grasp of every move on the political chess board, a breezy independence, and plenty of common sense, which has sometimes been described as genius in its working dress"[85].

On the home front Cook and his family were on the move again this time to an imposing little orchard farm on Windsor Road in the Baulkham Hills, a large fruit growing district[86]. By now the Cooks possessed another three children making a total of nine, all of which incidentally had been born prematurely. The last three children, two boys and a girl, were named Cecil, Raymond and Connie (or Constance)[87] respectively. Joseph continued to be the devoted husband and father although perhaps by now having inclined to greater leniency. Still deeply religious, he and his family attended Church whenever possible. He continued to preach or speak at anniversaries, services, and other Church functions including the Methodist conferences. In all his public life Cook never forgot his obligation and debt to the Church and always supported the Methodist cause.

Life was good for the Honourable Joseph Cook. He had come a long way from Silverdale in more ways than one.

4.   Fusion

Shortly after Cook had assumed leadership of the Opposition a Labor administration under Andrew Fisher collapsed after having only survived for six months. As a consequence, the Governor-General called on Alfred Deakin, leader of the Protectionists, to form a Government. Deakin, a lawyer and journalist had, in fact, been Prime Minister on two previous occasions i.e. 1903-4 and 1905-8. After somewhat protracted negotiations a fusion was formed between Deakin's protectionist group (otherwise known as Deakinite

Liberals), Cook's free-trade group and the 'Corner' group (Conservative protectionists) led by Sir John Forrest. Deakin was elegantly tall, slightly stooped and commanded attention. Cook once likened him to a 'beautiful, stately but timid giraffe'[88]. Nevertheless, to Deakin's credit and the manner in which he handled the extremely delicate negotiations, the Deakin-Cook (or Fusion) administration took office on 2nd June 1909[89] with Deakin as Prime Minister and Cook as Deputy Leader and Defence Minister. It was during this period that he did his most noteable work as a Minister of the Crown.

Terrible scenes followed in the House during the induction of the Fusion Cabinet which culminated in the tragic death of the Speaker. As a consequence of having formed the coalition Deakin had to bear bitter insults from such persons as Sir William Lyne, one of his former Ministers, who openly called him Judas, and Labor's irascible William Hughes who poured scorn on him[90]. The Speaker, Sir Frank Holder, attempted to keep the factions in order but at 5 o'clock in the morning, during an all night sitting, he had a seizure whilst in the Chair and this proved fatal a few hours later[91]. Nevertheless, despite the tragic start to their term of office, the Deakin-Cook administration was one of the most successful in federal politics and, in fact, Deakin is regarded by some as the outstanding political personality of the first period of the Commonwealth[92].

Cook served Deakin loyally just as he did when serving under Reid in the New South Wales Legislative Assembly a decade before and Deakin increasingly appreciated Cook's loyalty and unwavering support. Cook, no doubt, became influenced by Deakin and, in particular, by his oratorical style. Deakin had always captivated his audiences and was by repute the most inspiring speaker of his day, regarded by admirers as 'the silver tongued orator' or 'the supreme word spinner'[93].

Cook by now was firmly of the opinion that no class of society should benefit at the expense of another and that there should be no unnecessary restrictions on personal freedom. He considered all Labor policies to be sectional and socialist, whilst his own were liberal and in the national interest. Continuing to attack the Labor pledge and its organisation he was also strongly critical of their policies whenever given an opportunity. He had a thorough grasp of political manoeuvring[94] but his style of speech mellowed as he gradually lost the preacher's style of delivery doubtless due to having been influenced, to a certain extent, by colleagues such as Deakin. One characteristic of the old style did remain, however, as he continued to make great use of his hands when speaking in public or in Parliamentary debates[95].

Ever since the conception of the Commonwealth, Australian Governments had debated the question of defence and the security of the Pacific. Politicians had also discussed the possibility of the formation of an independent Australian navy, particularly after Japan's significant victory over Russia in 1905 when the latter's naval fleet had been destroyed. Australians began to express concern about their apparent vulnerability and at the rapid rise of Japan as an expansionist power in the Pacific, Cook himself in Parliament in 1905 had commented that 'we are all coming to recognise more and more our vulnerability to attack from the east'[96]. Further, events in Europe in 1908-9, when the major powers finalised their war mobilisation plans and Britain decided to outmatch the German naval programme, persuaded the British Government and the Admiralty that there was some merit in the argument that Australia should be allowed to develop its own naval force.

Events in the Pacific had also persuaded many Australians that their existing system of military defence was inadequate. Consequently Deakin requested Lord Kitchener to visit Australia and advise on military requirements. Unfortunately he was not able to accept the invitation immediately and so on 21st September 1909 Cook introduced a bill providing for compulsory military training[97].

On such an occasion Cook took the opportunity to give Parliament a comprehensive survey of the Government's defence policy and to set out fully the strategic reasoning behind it. He referred to the 'development of armed forces in the Pacific region and the unequal distribution of these forces'. He also compared naval strengths noting that 'while Japan had 15 battleships and America 1 battleship and 11 cruisers in the Pacific, Britain was represented, in terms of capital ships, by only 4 outdated cruisers'[98]. Cook also referred to the fact that Japan had an army of 2 or 3 million of the best trained troops in the world and that 'Australia is the most distant, the richest and at the same time, the most vulnerable part of the British Empire'[99].

On the question of naval defence, Cook persuaded the House to endorse an agreement which had been reached earlier that year at the Imperial Defence Conference in London for the creation of an Australian naval squadron built and financed from Australian resources. Subsequently the best advice was sought as to which class of vessels would be required and the necessary orders placed for their construction in Britain. The first ship of the Australian navy, the destroyer "Parramatta", was launched on the Clyde in February 1910 and reached Australia in November of that year[100].

Returning to the question of military defence, Cook's bill proposed compulsory training of males from 14 - 20 years of age. They were to undergo training for 16 days per year and subsequently remain on the active list, by means of one day annual musters, until they were 26[101]. The scheme was, however, to be reviewed following Kitchener's report on Australia's military needs. It was estimated that the measures proposed would provide a first and second line military force of 66,000 men[102].

Subsequently, Lord Kitchener did visit Australia and Cook accompanied him on his tour of inspection[103]. In his report, Kitchener recommended that a military force of 80,000 troops was required for Australia's defences as opposed to the 66,000 originally proposed. Eventually steps were taken to implement this by extending the age limit for compulsory training to 25 years. Other recommendations adopted included the creation of a military college primarily to train officers and this was established at Duntroon[104].

As one might have expected the defence programme cut across all parties' policies. The subject was paramount and Labor debated the Defence Bill virtually without tactical opposition. Further to aid the defence programme Cook authorised the establishment of a small arms factory at Lithgow and others for the production of uniforms and military equipment.

The life of the Deakin-Cook administration was cut short by a sweeping Labor victory in the elections held in April 1910. Labor secured 42 seats in the lower house of 75 and 23 out of the 36 in the senate[105]. Deakin had pushed through a surprising amount of legislation during his third, but brief, period of office, almost all of which was in accord with the nationalist tradition[106]. The setting up of an Australian High Commission in London had also been authorised and George Reid was appointed as the first High Commissioner.

Cook was returned in those elections but reverted to the opposition benches once again. However he did have the satisfaction of seeing Labor, under Andrew Fisher, carrying to a successful conclusion the establishment of an Australian navy and defence force. As a consequence, by 1914, Australia had established an autonomous system of military training which was intended to create an army of citizen-soldiers and a system of naval defence which could, in time of war, be integrated with the British navy.

Meanwhile, back in England, on 17th August 1911 Cook's mother Margaret died aged 80[107]. She had been living at Atherton near Manchester for some time, alternating between the homes of her daughters, Caroline and Emily (now Mrs.Lord and Mrs.Taylor respectively) who ran a successful millinery business there. She died at 190 Stanley Street, the residence of Emily[108]. Margaret Cooke was a very dignified lady, renowned for her lace caps and collars which she constantly wore and was highly respected in the Atherton community, just as she had been at Silverdale. People frequently enquired as to her well being and called on her to present floral tributes of which she was very fond. In fact Emily's residence was adjacent to a park and each day the park keeper called with fresh flowers for her[109]. Her death came as a major blow to her eldest son when the news reached him in Australia some weeks later. For the rest of his life Joseph never ceased to speak in the highest terms of his mother and acknowledged the great debt he owed to her[110]. Although Margaret Cooke was fortunate in knowing that her son had been a Minister of the Crown and had some success in Australian politics, she was never able to share with him the greater successes that he had later in life. She was buried at Atherton.

Returning to Australia and the political scene, the surviving fusionists formed themselves into the Liberal Party[111] under the leadership of Alfred Deakin. However in 1913 ill health forced Deakin to resign. On 20th January Deakin presided over a gathering at Parliament House of 39 members of the party who proceeded to hold a ballot to decide the new leader. A first ballot left Cook and Sir John Forrest as contenders, the former eventually winning by one vote[112].

Shortly after the leadership election the editor of the Cumberland Argus and Fruitgrowers' Advocate commented that Cook had practically been the leader for the past two Parliamentary sessions as a result of Deakin's illness. Whilst regretting Deakin's illness, the editor further observed that "Mr.Cook will as he becomes more widely known throughout the Commonwealth inspire the people's confidence in him as now the fit and proper person to lead and still more the right man in the right place when he becomes the next Liberal Prime Minister." That same edition noted that owing to Cook's 'insistence and organising ability' New South Wales would have a fairer distribution of seats in the next federal elections[113].

That year was not uneventful to say the least for the Hon.Joseph Cook (or Jo-Cook as he had generally become known[114]). There was a certain amount of unrest within the Liberal party membership following Cook's success in the leadership elections. Some of the Liberal-Protectionists were concerned that a former Free-Trader had become elected party leader. However, to his credit there was no party split and Cook marshalled his party for the forthcoming elections. By the time of the elections the Liberal party, if not entirely solid, was fully united under Cook's leadership.

The elections were held on 31st May, being a straight contest between Labor and Liberal. Labor's policies proposed a rapid centralisation of power in the Federal Parliament and an increase in the activities of Government in the community whereas the Liberals advocated the decentralisation of federal power and that governments should govern, not socialise[115]. Incidentally Labor had previously held two referendums, in 1911 and 1913, on proposals to give the Federal Government power over much of the nation's economic and industrial activities i.e. corporations, all trade and commerce, employment and wages etc. There had not been a majority in favour of the proposals at either referendum, the Liberals opposing them[116].

Cook in a policy speech at Parramatta on 3rd April undertook, amongst other things, to support increased immigration, place social services on a basis of national contributory insurance and reintroduce postal voting, previously abolished by Labor[117]. The Liberals felt the restoration of postal voting to be of importance as certain affluent members of the electorate, particularly females, considered it beneath their dignity to go to the polls. Labor shared this view, this being the reason for their having abolished postal voting!

Cook was once more successful in retaining his Parramatta seat, securing a majority in excess of 11,000 votes[118]. More than that, however, as the national results were becoming known the Governor-General, Lord Denman, called on him to form a Government[119]. As a consequence, on 24th June a Cabinet was sworn in with Cook as Prime Minister, he also taking the Home Affairs portfolio[120]. The former pit boy had attained the highest office in Commonwealth politics. He was now 53 years of age and 28 years had elapsed since he had left Silverdale.

Notes

1   Lloyds List

2   It should be noted, however, that excursions were
     being run from Silverdale station to the North
     Wales coast from as early as 1868.

3   Cumberland Argus & Fruitgrowers' Advocate, 8th
     February 1913

4   Australian Dictionary of Biography Melbourne 1966
     & Mrs.C.Bright. op.cit. p.269

5   J.Murdoch 'Joseph Cook'. University of New South
     Wales. Ph.D. Dissertation 1968. p.27

6   Cumberland Argus & Fruitgrowers' Advocate, 8th
     February 1913

7   Ex. info. Mrs.D.Holroyde

8   Birth certificate (Wolstanton Registration
     District)

9   Ex. info. Commander & Mrs.M.Hayward & Mrs.M.Wood

10   Mrs.C.Bright. op.cit. p.274

11   American Council of Learned Societies Dictionary
     of American Biography (section concerning
     R.W.Emerson) 1944

12   Ibid

13   Lithgow Mercury, 15th January 1904

14   Ibid

15   Daily Telegraph (Sydney) 3rd April 1890

16   J.Murdoch. op.cit. p.29

17   Sydney Morning Herald. 12th May 1860

18   R.Gollan. The Coal Miners of New South Wales.
     1963. p.20

19   Mrs.C.Bright. op.cit. p.270

20   R.Gollan. op.cit. p.22

21   Evening News (Sydney) 11th July 1888

22   Daily Telegraph (Sydney) 30th June 1891. See also
      Report of the Royal Commission on Strikes.   Sydney
      1891

23   R.Gollan. op.cit. p.10

24   Ibid

25   The Australian official spelling is used
      throughout this work

26   Cumberland Argus & Fruitgrowers' Advocate, 8th
      February 1913

27   Mrs.C.Bright. op.cit. p.270

28   Ibid

29   J.Murdoch. op.cit. p.47

30   Katoomba Times & Blue Mountaineer, 20th June 1891

31   'How an election is run' in Life magazine 15th
      October 1906

32   J.Murdoch. op.cit. p.48

33   Sydney Morning Herald, 17th June 1891

34   J. Niland. 'The birth of the movement for an
      eight hour working day in NSW' in Australian
      Journal of Politics & History. Vol.XIV 1968.
      pp.85/86

35   R.Gollan. op.cit. p.49

36   Daily Telegraph (Sydney) 30th June 1891

37   Mrs.C.Bright. op.cit. p.270

38   Ex. info. Mrs.D.Holroyde

39   Ex. info. Commander & Mrs.M.Hayward & Mrs.M.Wood.
      J.A. La Nauze in his book Alfred Deakin also
      refers to Cook's shorthand ability

40   B.Dickey. Politics in New South Wales 1856 -
      1900. 1969 p.180

41   M.H.Ellis. op.cit. p.20

42   B.Dickey. op.cit. p.181

43   M.H.Ellis. op.cit. p.20

44   Ex. info. Mrs.D.Holroyde

45   Katoomba Times and Blue Mountaineer, 6th October 1893

46   Sydney Morning Herald, 6th August 1894

47   J.Murdoch. op.cit. p.417

48   Daily Telegraph (Sydney) 5th April 1895

49   Daily Telegraph (Sydney) 26th August 1896

50   Ibid

51   Mrs.C.Bright. op.cit. p.273

52   Ibid p.274. See also Daily Telegraph (Sydney) 26th August 1896

53   J.Murdoch. op.cit. p.97

54   Ibid p.96

55   Ex. info. Mrs.M.Wood (who kindly supplied a copy of his credentials for this post)

56   Daily Telegraph (Sydney) 22nd October 1898

57   The Dominions & Independencies of the Empire ed. H.Gunn 1924

58   A.W.Martin 'The Legislative Assembly of NSW 1856 - 1900' in Australian Journal of Politics & History Vol.II. 1956. p.66

59   G.H.Reid My reminiscences. 1917. p.189

60   Ex. info. Mrs.D.Holroyde

61   J.Murdoch op.cit. pp.106 & 414

62   Ex. info. Mrs.M.Wood

63   Cumberland Argus & Fruitgrowers' Advocate, 8th February 1913

64   Ex. info. Mrs.D.Holroyde

65   Ex. info. Mrs.D.Holroyde & Mrs.J.Fearnley

66   Ex. info. Rev.E.G.Clancy

67   Sydney Morning Herald, 25th January 1894

68   _Ibid_ 23rd January 1894

69   _Ibid_ 22nd January 1895

70   Ex. info. Rev. E.G.Clancy

71   J.Murdoch. op.cit. p.129

72   G.Sawer _Australian Federal Politics & Law 1901 – 1929_. 1972 p.1

73   _Ibid_ p.4

74   Ed. F.Crowley _A new history of Australia_. 1974. p.264

75   J.Murdoch. op.cit. p.136 (see also M.H.Ellis. _op.cit_. p.20)

76   _Australian Dictionary of Biography_ Melbourne 1966

77   J.Murdoch. op.cit. p.136

78   Ex. info. Mrs.J.Fearnley

79   _The Methodist_, 9th August 1947

80   F.Crowley. _op.cit_. p.261

81   _Commonwealth Parliamentary Debates_ 17:6280

82   G.H.Reid. _op.cit_. p.239

83   _Ibid_ p.239

84   _Ibid_ p.261

85   M.H.Ellis. _op.cit_. p.21

86   Ex. info. Mrs.M.Wood (see also M.H.Ellis. _op.cit_. p.21)

87   Ex. info. Mrs.R.F.Cook. Mrs.J.Fearnley & Mrs.D.Holroyde

88   N.Meaney _The Search for Security in the Pacific 1901-14_. 1981. p.206

89   G.Sawer op.cit. p.66

90   M.H.Ellis. _op.cit_. p.22. See also G.Greenwood. _Australia – a social and political history_. 1955. p.224

91   G.H.Reid. _op.cit_. p.265

92   G.Greenwood. op.cit. p.216

93   F.Crowley. op.cit. p.267

94   Australian Dictionary of Biography (entry on Cook)
      1966

95   Ex. info. Mrs.D.Holroyde

96   Commonwealth Parliamentary Debates. August 1905
      (XXVI 1624)

97   N.Meaney. op.cit. p.188

98   Ibid p.188

99   Ibid p.188

100   F.Crowley. op.cit. p.294

101   N.Meaney. op.cit. p.188

102   Ibid p.189

103   Ex. info. Mrs.D.Holroyde (see also Alfred Deakin
      by J.A. La Nauze. p.586)

104   F.Crowley. op.cit. p.295

105   G.Greenwood. op.cit. p.226

106   Ibid p.224

107   Death certificate (Leigh Registration District)

108   Ex. info. Mrs.D.Holroyde (also death certificate)

109   Ex. info. Mrs.D.Holroyde

110   The Methodist, 9th August 1947

111   See Round Table (London) August 1911 edition for
      definition - "To avoid misunderstanding, it should
      be pointed out that the term 'Liberal' is
      frequently used in Australia to denote the whole
      body of those opposed to the Labour, or Socialist
      policy, and includes not only persons to whom the
      name would be given in England but also many who
      in that country would be called Conservatives or
      even Tories". p.502

112   J.A. La Nauze Alfred Deakin. 1966 pp.624/5

113   Cumberland Argus and Fruitgrowers' Advocate. 8th
      February 1913

114   M.H.Ellis. op.cit. p.20

115   F.Crowley. op.cit. p.308

116   Ibid p.308

117   G.Sawer. op.cit. p.111

118   J.Murdoch. op.cit. p.242

119   Sentinel, 21st June 1913

120   G.Sawer. op.cit. p.113

-bout 'Hallelujah' and did so After
which I dropped out of the ranks and
entered a Chinese quarter of the city

WHAT FREE-TRADE HAS DONE FOR ENGLAND.

Done—for Englishmen !

TO THE EDITOR OF "THE AUSTRALIAN STAR."

Sir,—I have just read with interest in
your columns the letter contributed by C
O Waldow, and its uncertain tone re unemployed, &c, makes me feel that I would
like to write you a short chapter of English experience, for, after all, we can
tell more confidently those things we
have seen and felt R unemployed
of England, your correspondent thinks
"there may be 700,000" I am per-
fectly sure he is under the mark The
unemployed in England at this moment
are considerably over 1,000,000 But, sir
the number of unemployed is not the only
index to Free-trade disaster. I would
very much rather take the position of
those who are employed as indicating the
results of any fiscal policy The
HERALD writer says "there may
be plenty of work, if labour would
accept the wages which capital is able
to pay." Let us see A large firm of
iron manufacturers in Staffordshire has
just ceased operations, the sole reason
assigned being their inability to compete
with Belgian iron. The employees of the
firm have had their wages reduced to 10
per cent., and for the last 12 months there
have been able-bodied men employed in
and around the blast furnaces, working 10
to 12 hours per day for the small pit-
tance of 2s 6d These men have sub-
mitted to reduction after reduction
rather than take the risk of finding
employment in a country where it was so
scarce, and now they are compelled to do
it, for with these reduced wage rates they
are not able to compete with the foreign
article This is not hear-say it is a hard
fact, and it is one amongst many The
above county is noted for its production of
iron, and I know from personal experience
that the mills of the whole county do not
run more than six months of the year.

The figures re pauperism of England are
misleading Nearly the whole industrial
population of England are, at this
moment, living lives bordering on the
verge of starvation They would rather
starve than be dubbed paupers I have
seen with my own eyes men with pretty
constant work, steady and skilled, die
like rats from sheer starvation, and all
because of the decline of the export
trade, and the increase in the imported
article. Let me give one more fact to
illustrate what is transpiring every day in
Free-trade England A large colliery owner has just put down
a large shaft, at a cost, all told
of about £80,000 He had to st
80 yards through a loose, wet
sand-bed, and had to line it with tubing
He had a large ironworks of his own in
the vicinity of the shaft Yet, notwithstanding, he imported the whole of the

tubing from Belgium, at a cost of 15s per
ton cheaper than he could produce it in
his own works, and when spoken to
some of the workmen, who at that time
were working two days per week, he com-
placently remarked he was buying in the
cheapest market, as a Free-trader should
do

Now according to the Free trade theory
of exchange, he had to sell as well as buy
which simply means that he had to pay
for the iron he bought in Belgium How
did he pay for it ? Why sir, he made the
fact of his having bought cheaper from
Belgium a lever by which to wring from
his workmen a reduction of 10 per cent
This is how Free-trade is constantly paying
for imports She sells her flesh and blood
aye, and pulls off the last pound," for
imports she can herself produce How are
we paying for our imports at the present
time ? Simply by selling our credit at an
enormous sacrifice, as well as our raw
materials at a dead loss According to the
Free trader we are doing grandly if we can
sustain our credit in a foreign land
It does not matter that our own hands
are compelled to take pretty bad deals
so long as they keep doing something to
sustain our credit in England Under-
lying all this is the assumption that we
must keep on borrowing in order to live
and unless we keep doing something to
sustain our credit, it will one day give out
The element of risk is clearly discernible in
the high interest we pay for our loans in
England The quality of our assets, railways, &c, is contingent upon the manufacturing prosperity of the country This
is prospective, hence the high interest We do sell, indeed We sell
at the last analysis, our flesh and blood
our independence, our credit, and per-
sistence in this kind of barter will lead to
ruinous results

The HERALD writer alludes to the " de-
generacy," " loss of independence" of the
British workman Here is a tacit admission of the baneful effects of the fiscal
policy upon the morals of the nation
There is "a loss of independence," and
why ? The soul of the worker is ground
completely out of him by the keen competition to which he is subjected

The mills of the Gods grind slowly,
But they grind exceeding small

The "tone" of their voice is not "whin-
ing" It is the cry of despair Their
'discontent" may be "unreasonable," but
it is forced on them by their extreme condition. Sir, a six months' residence
amongst the workers of England, at the
present, would teach the HERALD writer
more on this subject than he ever read, or
wrote But, ah me ! ' Ignorance is bliss '
Let him continue to write his Free-trade
platitudes. The workers of England cry
our for justice They will get it ere long
—let us hope by righteous and "reasonable" means.—Yours,

JOSEPH COOK

Lithgow, 28th December.

A PUZZLER '!

The following curious incident occurred the

Arrival in Australia

X   An early twentieth century view of the
industrial town of Lithgow, 100 miles from Sydney
in New South Wales, where Cook first settled in
1886, working in the Vale of Clwydd Colliery there.

XII   In 1901 Cook moved to Marrickville a middle-
class suburb just north of Botany Bay, in order to
more conveniently carry out his political duties
as member for the Parramatta constituency in the
Federal Parliament.

XIII   Summer Hill, the inner Sydney suburb, where
Cook resided during the years of mature political
office.

XIV The life of Arthur Hassam, childhood and life-long friend of Cook, showed a different pattern of career development. Remaining in England he became a distinguished Mining Engineer being honoured three times by the Mayoralty of Newcastle-under-Lyme. (1922-5)

III   Prime Minister and Statesman

1.   Prime Minister

In choosing the members of his Cabinet, Cook not only had regard for those who were likely to be absolutely loyal, but for colleagues who had previously held Ministerial office and those who, whilst perhaps lacking in experience, were considered to have ability.

Sir John Forrest, Cook's former opponent for the Liberal leadership and a former Premier of Western Australia (and a famous explorer) was chosen as deputy and also given the Treasury portfolio. The Cabinet also included the following:-

Sir William H. Irvine	Attorney - General
Senator E.D.Millen	Defence
P.M.Glynn	External Affairs
L.Groom	Trade & Customs
A.Wynne	Postmaster General
Senator J.H.McColl	Vice-President of the Executive Council
Senator J.S.Clemons	} Ministers without
W.H.Kelly	} portfolio

1

Irvine (Member for Flinders) a former Premier of Victoria, was a powerful debater, a distinguished lawyer and fiercely anti-Labor. Millen (New South Wales) a friend and colleague of Cook, was an experienced politician, a good speaker and party organiser. Glynn (Angas, South Australia) and Groom (Darling Downs, Queensland) were considered by Cook to be loyal and had already held Cabinet office whilst Wynne (Balaclava) and McColl (Victoria) were elderly, experienced politicians having served in Victoria State Cabinets. Clemons (Tasmania) and Kelly (Wentworth NSW) were loyal supporters of Cook, the latter also being a personal friend. Kelly was given the task of supervising the day to day running of the Home Affairs Department under Cook whilst McColl became responsible for the Electoral Department.

Shortly after taking office Cook welcomed the battle-cruiser 'Australia' and other vessels under the command of Admiral Patey to Australian waters and witnessed the realisation of the Australian navy, the establishment of which he had done so much to bring about. By 1914 Australia had achieved much in defence. Her naval unit was substantially completed and naval bases were being planned at Western Port, Victoria and Cockburn Sound, Western Australia. The Australian army was 46,000 strong and, in addition to the military training college at Duntroon, a flying school had been established at Point Cook. Australia, in fact, was the only Dominion to experiment with aviation for defence purposes before the first World War[2]. Much attention had also been given to fortifications, armaments and ammunition factories. However in May of that year, following a presentation to the Senate indicating the strength of British and foreign naval forces in the Pacific and showing a great discrepancy between Japanese and British forces, the Cook administration entered into negotiations with New Zealand for a joint Australasian fleet and also sought authorisation for an additional naval construction programme[3].

Cook, as Prime Minister, was concerned not only to have good working relationships with the Governor-General and the permanent Heads of the Government Departments but to behave at all times with proper decorum. His dealings with the two Governor-Generals, Lord Denman, and later Sir Ronald C.Munro Ferguson, were correct and beyond reproach. He advised them regularly and promptly of developments. Ferguson in comparing him with other Prime Ministers he had worked with wrote that Cook was "from a Governor-General's point of view, quite the best, for he was always anxious to be thoroughly constitutional in his relations with the King's representative and took pains to be 'correct' in every particular"[4]. He was equally successful in maintaining a good working relationship with the permanent Departmental Heads, having come to understand the art of delegation, something he had not perhaps fully grasped when serving as a Minister of the Crown under Reid prior to Federation.

Unfortunately life did not run so smoothly for Cook in Parliament as the Liberals only had a majority of one in the House of Representatives. The situation in the Senate was even worse as Labor held 22 of the 36 seats[5]. When Cook was forced to appoint a Speaker, Elliott Johnson, his majority in the House of Representatives melted away[6]. As a consequence, dependent upon the casting vote of the Speaker, and faced with a hostile Senate, the Government found itself unable to proceed with its legislative programme.

After the Senate had twice rejected Irvine's Government Preference Prohibition Bill, which sought to abolish preference to unionists in Government employment, Cook decided that the time had come when the deadlock should be broken[7]. Section 57 of the Commonwealth constitution provided for a dissolution of both Houses in certain circumstances. Consequently, on 4th June 1914 Cook wrote to the Governor-General, Sir Ronald Munro Ferguson, requesting a dissolution of both the House of Representatives and the Senate on the ground that he could not carry on because of the general state of deadlock between the two Houses. The Governor-General had only arrived in Australia a few weeks previously and, as the issue was somewhat complex, sought the advice of the Chief Justice, Sir Samuel Griffith. After some hesitation, the Governor-General agreed to accept Cook's request and the elections were subsequently arranged for the following September[8].

In the meantime events were happening in Europe which culminated in the outbreak of World War I or, as some described it, the war to end all wars - Armageddon! On 28th June at Sarajevo, capital of Bosnia, Archduke Franz Ferdinand, the heir to the Austrian throne was assassinated by Serbian terrorists. Later on 30th July, as Melbourne shivered in rain and sleet, the Australian press announced that Austria and Russia had mobilised[9]. In effect Austria had declared war on Serbia to seek revenge whilst Russia, allied to Serbia, had mobilised against Austria. The latter had been assured of Germany's support if she went to war against Russia[10] and thus on 2nd August Germany sent an ultimatum to the Belgium government demanding free passage for her troops. Belgium refused to allow its neutrality to be violated and consequently, two days later, German troops began to invade[11]. As a result of such action the British Government delivered a swift ultimatum demanding that Germany respect Belgian neutrality and when this was ignored Britain entered the war to sustain treaty obligations to Belgium and also to support France[12]. Germany had, in effect, declared war on France on 3rd August following an alleged incident involving the bombing by a French aviator of a railway line near Karlsruhe and Nuremburg[13].

On 5th August at 12.45 p.m. Cook announced to the press in his Melbourne office - "I have received the following despatch from the Imperial government - "war has broken out in Germany""[14]. The news was not altogether unexpected as cables had been passing between London and Melbourne for some days concerning the critical situation. Cook himself had learned on the previous evening that Britain was at war as he attended a country meeting in Victoria.

Shortly before the outbreak of war Cook had declared that "all our resources in Australia are ..... for the preservation and the security of the Empire". For the opposition, Labor's Andrew Fisher pledged that "Australians will stand beside our own to help and defend her (i.e. the Empire) to our last man and our last shilling"[15]. The Liberal government, now acting in a caretaker capacity, agreed to place the Australian naval squadron at the disposal of the British Admiralty and to despatch an expeditionary force of 20,000 men 'of any suggested composition to any destination desired by the Home Government'[16].

Within a few days of the declaration of war Cook arranged for a conference of State Premiers and Commonwealth Ministers to meet in Melbourne. This was a reflection of the government's anxiety to facilitate co-operation with the British Government. Although the Commonwealth was entrusted with the responsibility for defence, there was not, at that time, a clear definition of the powers it possessed in time of war. The conference dealt with a wide range of subjects and was later described by a historian as 'thoroughly satisfactory'[17]. Also, during this period Cook, at the request of the British Government, sent a force of 1,500 men to seize German wireless installations in the Pacific islands. The mission was a total success[18]. It is interesting to note that Cook in 1908, at the time when concern was being expressed about the expansion of German naval power had warned that "Germany was the British Empire's chief antagonist"[19].

In September, Cook was returned once again in the Parramatta constituency, but unopposed on this occasion[20]. However the Liberals were heavily defeated. Labor captured 42 of the 75 seats in the House of Representatives and 31 of the 36 in the Senate[21].

Due to its preoccupation with the deadlock situation the Liberal's legislative record was relatively small. In fact 27 Acts were passed of which 15 were routine financial measures and 6 were minor amendments[22]. 23 Bills were defeated, laid aside or lost, including the one proposing the restoration of postal voting (Postal Voting Restoration Bill 1913)[23]. The Liberals did have some important legislative achievements but these in the main were of a substantially non-party character regarding the organisation of government.

In retrospect, Cook was more than aware that his administration's record was not an inspiring one, but at the same time when the results of the 1913 elections were known he must have appreciated that the ensuing Parliament was likely to be unworkable. Although the Liberals could have obtained a dissolution of the House of Representatives at some reasonable time, this would have been of little value to them since, had they been successful in the ensuing election, there would still have been difficulty with the passage of legislation through the Senate which Labor controlled with a large majority. Thus to the Cook administration the only satisfactory solution was a double dissolution.

After the dissolution had been announced Cook had worked untiringly for the Liberals to achieve success in the election but this had been overshadowed by the outbreak of World War I which transformed the whole Australian political scene. Not only having been involved in the hustings but also in directing Australia's war effort, albeit for a brief, but important, period, put him under great strain. Having to sleep at his Melbourne office at times, it was not unknown for him to work an 18 hr. day[24]. Cook was an incredible man, seemingly to have boundless energy. More than one historian has described him as 'untiring'. On this occasion, however, the fact that he had driven himself so much took its toll and he returned home to the Baulkham Hills to Mary and the children to recuperate.

Cook's period as Prime Minister is marked, amongst other things, by the naming of the suburb of Cook in Canberra after him, this being the custom for all Prime Ministers of the Commonwealth[25]. Also in this capacity he planted an oak tree in a park at Falconbridge in the Blue Mountains. I'm told that Cook's tree is 'the most noble of them all and grows straight and true'. A street is also named after him in the Baulkham Hills[26].

So Cook's brief period as Prime Minister, just 15 months, was over and he was never to hold the post again. His political career, however, was far from finished. He returned to the Opposition benches though now as a member of His Majesty's Privy Council, his first public honour. The Governor-General told him "I always think that as the VC is the prize of the military, so is the PC that of civil life"[27]. Having fully recovered his energies he directed himself to the war effort. The first steps had been taken to implement Australia's commitment to the war effort and Labor, under Andrew Fisher, continued the task.

2.   War!

As a result of defence decisions taken in earlier years, Australia was able to make a substantial contribution to the war effort when hostilities commenced. The Australian naval squadron was soon in action and proving its worth by adding security to the shipping lanes and also in seeking out the German Pacific naval squadron which it eventually destroyed following a fierce battle off the Falkland Islands. Furthermore the military college which had been established at Duntroon in 1911 was providing officers of quality. Australians flocked to the colours and by the end of the year over 50,000 men had enlisted[28]. Initial training for the troops was commenced in

Australia. However those to be first drafted overseas, with units of the New Zealand army, completed their training in Egypt and went on to win renown at Gallipoli. The Anzacs (as the Australian & New Zealand Army Corps became known) went on later to distinguish themselves at the first offensive on the Somme and later at the bloody battles at Ypres and Passchendaele, names which will never be forgotten!

Following the election defeat Cook was re-elected Liberal party leader. Shortly after the opening of Parliament, in the House of Representatives, he confirmed his party's support to the Government in the war effort by saying that "we shall be behind them most cordially with our best support, and not critical support, in prosecuting this war right to the end and in financing it to the full in every legitimate and reasonable way"[29]. The prime concern of both Government and Opposition was to defeat Germany and for the war to be brought to a successful conclusion as quickly as possible. Labor were desperately concerned to contribute maximum assistance to the war effort and the Liberals were resolute in giving every encouragement. Cook led his party in supporting recruiting drives endeavouring to encourage every available man to enlist. He urged his fellow countrymen - "let us gird up our loins and address ourselves anew to the task and meet all that is to come"[30]. In that same speech he commented that Britain had called 3 million men to the colours and that so far Australia had sent a little over 60,000 men to the war. He urged, 'at the risk of incurring unpopularity and odium' that Australia should aim at keeping 2 army corps effectively in the field. He continued "we should fix a definite objective in our mind of 100,000 men in the fighting line ...., with continual reinforcements to keep up their effective strength. Also we should be very grateful that at last the Small Arms Factory is not closing its gates at 12 o'clock on Saturdays after one shift. To work our munition factories in war time on these conditions suggests that we ought to ask the Germans to cease firing while we have our holidays and have our rest. The thing would be a farce, if it were not a tragedy. Unceasing and unresting should be our aim until victory has been achieved. In addition, there is need of a thorough mobilisation of all our resources both in the civil, social, and military spheres..... There is only one way to win this war and that is by absolute unity of soul and purpose throughout the whole Empire"[31].

In October 1915 Prime Minister Andrew Fisher resigned to succeed Sir George Reid as High Commissioner in London. The Attorney-General, William Morris Hughes then became Prime Minister. Shortly afterwards in France, British casualties rose towards 1,000,000 and

Britain looked to her Colonies and Dominions for replacements. As a consequence, their Prime Ministers were invited to discuss the progress of the war and Hughes arrived in London in March 1916[32]. Hughes also took the opportunity of visiting the Western Front in France by which time he was convinced that, for the allies to be successful, Australia would have to increase its supply of men and munitions.

By this time the British Government had introduced conscription[33] and the Imperial General Staff had decided to move the Anzacs from Egypt to the Western Front for a major offensive.

Hughes returned to Australia convinced that the only method of providing the necessary additional manpower was by means of conscription. This gave rise to differences of opinion in his Cabinet, the Labor Party and the Labor movement and, in fact, the country split into two opposing camps. However, after a struggle, Hughes obtained the necessary approval for a referendum on the issue. Cook and the Liberals for their part also shared the view that conscription was the only feasible method by which Australia could fulfill its commitments[34]. The referendum was held on 28th October 1916 and on that day the Sydney Morning Herald carried a message from the Prime Minister in Nelsonian terms - "Australia expects that every man and woman will this day do their duty and vote YES!" Despite this the result indicated that 1,087,557 voted for and 1,160,037 voted against the issue[35]. As a consequence, shortly afterwards, following an attempt to move a vote of no confidence in his leadership, Hughes lead his supporters from a meeting of the Parliamentary Labor party at Melbourne. He subsequently announced the formation of a National Labor Party and formed a second administration from those who had remained loyal to him.

At the first opportunity in Parliament, Labor's new leader, Frank G.Tudor, moved a vote of no confidence to test the position of the Hughes administration. However, having carefully weighed up the situation, the Liberals decided to pledge conditional support to the Government which Cook confirmed to the House on 29th November[36]. Although some Liberals were in favour of a general election, the majority considered that supporting the Government was a necessary patriotic step. Cook wrote in his diary "we should make war on Germany - not on ourselves and one another. We should agree and get on with the war"[37]. Having taken such step, however, Cook came under pressure to negotiate a fusion. Negotiations were, in fact, commenced following which in February 1917, Hughes reconstituted the Government, with six portfolios going to the Liberals and five going to his own supporters. Cook was appointed Minister for the Navy[38]. (Hughes, in fact, retained the defence portfolio for George F.Pearce (later Sir) one of his supporters). Plans were subsequently put in hand for a general election.

Meanwhile in Europe the war was not progressing too well for the allies, the opposing front line trenches being static. The Australian divisions had been moved to France to replace heavy losses at Verdun and had also seen action at the Somme. Together with the British troops they had experienced in full the horrors of trench warfare and the terrible slaughter for limited territorial gains. The allies were preparing an offensive for the Spring, the target being the newly completed, heavily fortified, Hindenburg (or Seigfried) line. The Australian Imperial Force (AIF) which was entrenched in mud near Baupaume eventually succeeded in taking a section of the German fortifications but at the expense of heavy casualties[39]. Such inhuman combat placed manpower demands upon Australia which, in turn, caused the controversy of conscription for overseas war service to grow. The numbers enlisting had declined and a general feeling of war weariness manifested itself. However every effort was continued to encourage Australians to volunteer for service.

Wives and mothers were urged to encourage their men to enlist, many females themselves enlisting as service nurses. Organisations were also set up to provide aid for the returning sick and wounded service personnel. Cook's wife, Mary, became very active in the Red Cross organisation to which she devoted considerable time and energy[40]. The Cook's eldest son, George Sydney, enlisted shortly after the outbreak of war. Having suffered serious head wounds during action at Gallipoli he went on to have a distinguished war service. Their second son, Albert, also saw action with the AIF on the Western Front[41]. The Cook's third son, Joseph William, was commissioned as a Second Lieutenant in the 5th Battalion North Staffords, a regiment from his parents' former County in England. He saw action with his regiment particularly in the trenches at Ransart, near Arras. He was promoted to the rank of Lieutenant, then Captain, before being transferred to another English regiment[42]. Joseph and Mary Cook, who incidentally by now had moved to Liverpool Road in the inner Sydney suburb of Summer Hill,[43] naturally endured much worry and anxiety over their sons' welfare during this period. Unlike some families, they were most fortunate that the Great War did not take the lives of any of their children.

3.   Return to Staffordshire

The general election was arranged for 5th May 1917 and was to be a two cornered fight between Nationalists and Labor.   Both Hughes and Cook were doubtful of the outcome, being equally convinced that they may lose votes to electors who were anti-conscriptionists. However Hughes in a speech at Sydney on 4th April stressed that winning the war was his party's major policy.   Whilst pledging to respect the verdict of the electorate on conscription for overseas service, he said that if the war situation demanded it, he would submit a proposal for a second referendum on the issue[44].

The election result was a resounding victory for the Nationalists.   In the House of Representatives they held 53 of the 75 seats, and all 18 vacancies in the Senate[45].   All Ministers were returned and the Hughes Nationalist administration continued in office.   Being returned for the Parramatta constituency with a majority of over 17,000[46] Cook retained the Navy portfolio.   All Cook's supporters were also re-elected.   Shortly after the election the Australian Nationalist Party was formed as many felt by then that it was unnecessary to continue as two individual groups (i.e.   in effect, National Labor & Liberal).   Hughes was elected party leader and Cook as deputy,[47] a post he was to hold for nearly 5 years.

Hughes, like Cook was an immigrant, born in London of Welsh parents.   Following a variety of jobs he studied law and was admitted to the Bar in 1903. Affectionately known to the public as 'Billy', Hughes was a 'hail fellow well met' in public life, always smiling and jolly[48].   On the floor of the House, however, he could be volatile and completely ruthless with critics, dissenters or oppositionists[49].   Although scrawny of body, a chronic sufferer from dyspepsia and deafness he was nevertheless extremely active in mind and body.   Hughes and Cook were completely opposite in temperament and this led to disagreements in Cabinet. Cook favoured a slower and constructive approach to problems whereas Hughes was inclined to be impetuous and lacking in tolerance.   However, Cook's behaviour towards Hughes was exactly the same as it had been when he had served under Reid and Deakin, that of unswerving loyalty, and self-effacement in the comparatively minor office of Navy Minister[50].   He even came to admire Hughes' strong leadership, immense energy and ingenuity, but there was never the same friendly relationship as there had been with Reid and Deakin.   In private Cook referred to Hughes as 'the little devil!'[51].

Against a background of news of further bloodbaths on the Western Front, together with a decline in the recruiting figures, Hughes announced his intention to hold a second referendum on the conscription issue. Feelings ran high as a consequence, resulting in the Prime Minister being pelted with eggs in Queensland. The Roman Catholic Archbishop of Melbourne, Dr.Daniel Mannix, denounced Hughes as a 'little Czar'[52]. The Archbishop whilst being desirous of the allies being the victors, nevertheless felt that Australia had already made sufficient sacrifices. He was not alone in this respect. Subsequently the referendum was held on 20th December. The question put to the voters was "Are you in favour of the proposal of the Commonwealth Government for reinforcing the Australian Imperial Forces overseas?". The result was 1,015,159 voted yes, whilst 1,181,747 voted no[53]. Before the poll Hughes had declared that his Government could not continue in office unless it was given a mandate to conscript and on 8th January 1918 he tendered his resignation but gave no advice to the Governor-General as to what to do. The latter having explored the situation, however, concluded that it would be improper to dissolve Parliament, it having been in existence for only 9 months and considered that he had no choice but to call upon Hughes to form another Government. In a memorandum to Parliament he explained that he felt that Hughes "had the best prospect of securing unity among his followers and of therefore being able to form a Government having those elements of permanence so essential to the conduct of affairs during war"[54]. Accordingly, two days later Hughes returned to office with exactly the same Cabinet as had resigned two days earlier![55]

In the meantime Cook had been seeking to reform the Naval Department. On taking office he had been concerned at its organisation and the apparent lack of co-ordination between sections. Conscious of his lack of knowledge of naval administration he requested Admiral J.R.Jellicoe, Commander of the Grand Fleet, to visit Australia and report on the matter. This was eventually agreed but by the time the report of Jellicoe's findings was received Cook was no longer in a position to effect any changes as he had moved to the Treasury[56]. Cook frequently deputised for Hughes in Parliament at this period and supervised Government business in the House. Hughes was thus able to attend to the enormous amount of business requiring his attention as Prime Minister and Attorney-General and he only attended Parliament for question times or to make a speech. Hughes' lack of attendance, however, caused Sydney's Daily Telegraph to comment that "to the House itself Mr.Cook appears to be the real leader. He has from his constant oversight of the business an intimate knowledge of everything that occurs and he is certainly exercising a direct force that should properly belong to the Prime Minister"[57].

In April Cook travelled with Hughes to London to represent Australia at the Imperial War Conference. W.A.Watts was appointed Acting Prime Minister in Hughes absence[58]. On their arrival in England Cook told representatives of the media that he was "delighted to see these shores again"[59]. Hughes, referring to the war effort, added that "all things were going well in Australia for the allies when he left. There was a feeling of staunch loyalty to the Mother Country and the allied cause. Recruits were rolling up and there was a continuous flow of men to the seat of war. They were the best type of Australians. He hoped that the present system of recruiting in Australia would achieve all that was expected from it"[60].

On learning of Cook's arrival Members of Wolstanton Urban District Council, the local authority serving Silverdale, his birth place, decided to arrange a civic reception in his honour and a Sub-Committee was duly appointed to make the necessary arrangements[61]. In the meantime, Cook had been making contact with his relatives and friends, including Arthur Hassam, by now a successful consulting mining and civil engineer with his own company, and had been invited to stay with him and his family in Newcastle-under-Lyme[62]. He also took time off to visit his parents' graves at Atherton and Silverdale respectively.

In between sessions of the Imperial War Conference both Cook and Hughes had discussions with British and allied politicians and had continual briefings on the war situation from officers of the AIF. On 28th June Cook was received by His Majesty, King George V, at Buckingham Palace[63]. He also attended a garden party at the Palace on 9th July[64].

On 3rd August it was formally announced that he was to have a knighthood conferred on him for services 'in high and confidential offices within His Majesty's colonial possessions and in reward for services rendered to the Crown in relation to the foreign affairs of the Empire'. The announcement coincided with the opening of Australia House in the Strand, London by the King and Queen Mary. Cook took a prominent part in the opening ceremony of the Commonwealth's new prestigious offices which was attended by his friend, Arthur Hassam, amongst others[65]. Cook became a Knight Grand Cross of the Order of St.Michael & St.George, the investiture taking place the following month, on September 26th at Buckingham Palace. A brass plate in the Chapel of the Order in St.Paul's Cathedral, London marks the occasion[66].

Cook was given a magnificent reception on his return to North Staffordshire and he was requested to attend a number of engagements. Shortly after his arrival in England he was requested to lay the foundation stone of the operating theatre at the North Staffs. Cripples Aid Society's hospital for children at "Longfields", Hartshill, Stoke-on-Trent. The Society had been founded some years before by Millicent, Duchess of Sutherland. At the special invitation of Mr.Sydney Malkin, who had taken a leading part in securing "Longfields" for a children's hospital, Cook paid a flying visit to the area to perform the ceremony on July 13th, staying as guest of the Hassam family. In his speech Cook referred to the number of Staffordshire people he had met in various parts of the world including a soldier, a Sergeant Major, wearing a Staffordshire Knot badge on his hat. Cook enquired about the badge whereupon the soldier asked if he knew anything of the Staffordshire Knot. Cook had replied that he did and the soldier added that he was born in Burslem. Cook replied "You don't pronounce it properly - its Boslum!" (this being the local dialect) which brought laughter from the audience. In a more serious vein according to the report in the media he dwelt on the fact that "the care of the children and our purpose in the war were parts of the same work for the best interests of humanity". He also ventured the opinion that the Kaiser should be deported as Napoleon was[67].

Cook, later that month, accompanied Hassam, being an elected Member of Staffordshire County Council, to a meeting of that authority. Seated with Lord Hatherton, the Chairman, Cook congratulated Members on the work they were doing. According to the report in the Weekly Sentinel he was fascinated with the agenda and the multitude of functions performed by the authority[68].

The next month Cook returned to North Staffordshire for a series of engagements, again staying as guest of Arthur Hassam. Hassam, like Cook, had lost his father at an early age (i.e. 7 years) and the two had originally become acquainted when working in the mines at Silverdale but they had also lived quite near to each other. They had pursued their friendship by regular correspondence since Cook had emigrated. As a result of a perforced rest due to injuries resulting from a roof fall at Silverdale Big Pit, Hassam decided to use the time to study for mining qualifications. Having qualified and having held posts at Bristol and in Yorkshire he returned to Staffordshire to hold a number of General Manager positions with colliery companies before eventually going into private practise[69]. Hassam, lived at "Glenmayne", a large Victorian semi-detached property set back from The Brampton, a tree lined road on the north eastern side of the town centre of Newcastle-under-Lyme. The road consisted largely of successful business men's residences and it is fair to say that the appearance of the area has altered little since that time. "Glenmayne" still exists, now the private residence of a doctor, and one can imagine Cook relaxing in the spacious gardens with Hassam and his family regaining his energies, before returning to the capital and the business of the Imperial War Conference.

On 4th September Wolstanton Urban District Council entertained Cook at a special luncheon at Broadmeadow School, Chesterton the event being presided over by the Council's Chairman, Mr.J.H.Woolliscroft. Many local dignitaries and guests attended the function including Cook's brothers and sisters. Cook was attended by his attaché, Commander J.G.Latham (later Chief Justice of Australia). After the welcoming speeches and congratulations on his knighthood Cook rose to speak. After the initial pleasantries he referred to the war in his old rousing pulpit style which no doubt, some had been waiting to hear - "This is not a war of armaments. This is not a war for arranging and negotiating and fixing up. It is a struggle of two conflicting ideals. You cannot negotiate a thing like that. There is only one thing you can do with it - either the light must drive out the darkness or it must be submerged by the darkness. One of these ideals is represented by light and the other by darkness and dour darkness at that.

Now, which is it to be? We have made up our minds in Australia, and you have made up your minds, and they have made up their minds in Canada and South Africa, and so from the north and the south, and the east and the west, troops have come, hurrying with swift feet to succour and to give help to the Motherland in this mighty struggle to preserve that dream of bygone days ..... And here we shall stay until every vestige of the enemy power has been defeated and trodden under foot for ever.

When that work of destruction has been accomplished, we say, further, that we shall rebuild the waste and we shall try to construct out of this chaos, this destruction of the war, a civilisation which shall be brighter and better than all that has gone before, and we shall try to make in the future an impossibility of ever having a war again of this character. We cannot afford another.

We have got to stop war in some way or another, in the interests of civilisation; and so this war is a different war than any in which our nation has been engaged in throughout the whole of history. It is a war for the end of wars; fighting that fighting may cease. "Why do our cannons roar? For a thousand years of peace?" I do not know whether we shall have a thousand years of peace as Harold Begbie so much desires in that little poem, but I believe we shall make it not worth the while of any nation in the immediate future to start another war of this sort.

Until that time is reached, we must combine all our forces and concentrate all our energies and stand "shoulder to shoulder and blade to blade" to conserve all that is best in the nation and all that is brightest and best in our civilisation. That is why I am here, glad to come back to my "ain folk" glad to meet so many of my friends of the earlier years, glad to meet all interested in the development of this country and who are interested as you all seem to be in the development of the new land from which I come, glad to be called a fellow-citizen of this mighty Empire and glad to tell you that the men and women of Australia are resolved in their desire and determination to fight with you for the successful ending of this war."

The report of the function in the <u>Sentinel</u> concludes with the words 'loud and continued applause!'[70]

Following the luncheon Arthur Hassam drove Cook to Silverdale and at the outskirts of the village they were met by the Silverdale Silver & Town Bands. They then proceeded in procession around the village to cheering crowds, including children, both village schools having been given a half day holiday in honour of the visit[71]. The procession passed Cook's former home in Newcastle Street and he recalled how he used to cross the fields at the rear of the property to court his intended bride at nearby Chesterton[72].

In the wet evening Cook attended a concert given in his honour at the Primitive Methodist Church in High Street where he was formerly a member of John Shenton's Bible Class[73]. Friends of his youth and other members of the chapel gave him a hearty reception. As he proceeded down the aisle to the rostrum an excited little man rose and greeted him in broad North Staffordshire dialect - "Hello Joe! dosna know mai, I'm owd Tom - ". Whether Cook knew his friendly assailant is not known, but he warmly shook him by the hand and did not bat an eyelid[74].

Following the event Cook expressed enthusiastic appreciation. He said that he had often told people in Australia of the high standard of singing in Silverdale and North Staffordshire. Mr.G.K.Downing in proposing a vote of thanks to Sir Joseph recalled there was another Joseph connected with the colonies and quoted what Pharaoh said to the Egyptians - "Go unto Joseph, what he saith to you, do!" - a remark which amused the audience[75].

The following morning, accompanied by his sisters Sarah and Emily, Cook returned to Silverdale to visit Mill Street school. Local author and friend, Harold Brown, was a pupil at that time and by coincidence occupied a desk with the writer's late uncle, Les Bebbington. He recalls Sir Joseph and his party being shown into the classroom by Frank Ellams, the headmaster. Looking extremely smart and dignified, reminiscent of King Edward VII, Cook spoke quietly to the pupils about his work and travels. Before leaving he signed the log book and wrote in a clear hand that he was 'very pleased with all I have seen and proud to visit the school'. His sisters also endorsed the entry.

In the afternoon at 3 p.m. Cook attended the Guildhall at Newcastle-under-Lyme where the Borough Council conferred upon him the Honorary Freedom of the Borough[76]. Having been welcomed by the Mayor, Councillor W.V.S.Gradwell Goodwin, the Town Clerk Joseph Griffith, read a eulogy (Illustration XXV).

The Council then unanimously resolved to admit Sir Joseph to be an Honorary Freeman of the Borough and the Corporate Seal of the Council was affixed to the address which was presented to him in the form of a scroll contained in a casket[77].

Cook in his acknowledgement speech remarked that he had often admired the Guildhall building as a young man but that he had only been inside once before. This, he said, to the amusement of the Councillors, was on the occasion that the Magistrates fined him 25/- in respect of his dog 'which broke bounds and was without a muzzle!' In a more serious vein he turned, inter alia, to the subject of local government - "My own impression of your system of local government is that of a very wonderful one and there is nothing that has filled me with so much admiration since coming into this country and looking into it as the wonderfully co-ordinated systems of Government with which you control the functions of the daily government of the people of this great country. Indeed I will go further and say that this self government is the secret of the Empire's success. It lies at the root and base of it all and without it this Empire could no longer be controlled. And after all, is it not the very essence of the democratic instinct of the time that the nearer you can take the government to the people of the country the more certain it is that it is better controlled and the more wisely it is ordained the more certain it is also that the more economically it is administered".

Following the ceremony a special dinner was held in Sir Joseph's honour in the Municipal Hall, in Ironmarket. Musical interludes were provided by

Mr.G.Bass's orchestra from Silverdale[78].

On 13th September he returned to Silverdale, this time to visit his old school. This no doubt gave him immense pleasure as he was also able to greet a friend and former fellow pupil, Caleb Yates, who was now the headmaster. The school log book records that Cook addressed pupils and staff for over twenty minutes recalling many incidents of his school days but also giving some account of his work and travels and of Australia and the work done in connection with the war. The log book also notes that Cook's memory was very keen! Mrs.D.Kelsall who was present at the school on that occasion remembers Cook as being 'very smart, tall, well made with a small beard - a very nice looking man with a kindly face'. He presented a framed portrait in sepia of himself to the school. She also recalls that all the children were 'spruced up' for the event and that they sang the National anthem and 'Rule Britannia' for their distinguished visitor which is confirmed by the log book.

Sir Joseph was again busy with engagements on the following day commencing with a special luncheon at the North Stafford Hotel in Stoke-on-Trent at which he was presented with a choice collection of Doulton ware by Lord Dartmouth on behalf of the pottery manufacturers.

In his address Cook recalled his temporary employment with the North Staffs. Railway Company at Fenton and proceeded, as usual, into a resounding speech about the war effort. However he also had some advice for the pottery manufacturers:-

"If this war has taught us one thing it has taught us to come together. It has taught us to find points of agreement and to sink points of difference. If we can do that for the safety of the nation in time of war why should we not do it in relation to those things that touch our trade and those of our ordinary every day concerns? Why not apply it to our economic relations? I think we can take counsel from our enemies in this respect. I would strongly urge that upon the pottery industry because I believe the pottery industry has a great future before it. I don't think the world can beat you in skill or individual initiative and response but the world may beat you in the application of co-operative action in these individual concerns of yours. You must get together and remember unity means strength, not merely in the moral attributes of mankind but strength in the economic position. The trade as a trade can do things for the trade that individuals cannot do." (Cook, no doubt, would have been pleased to learn that a number of pottery manufacturers have, in recent years, done as he advocated).

After the luncheon the party proceeded to a Red Cross Féte at Trentham Gardens, the former residence of the Duke and Duchess of Sutherland, where he made an appeal for funds on behalf of that organisation[79].

Cook's return to North Staffordshire was a resounding success far beyond any expectations that he may have had. The editor of the local Sentinel, Henry Barrett Green, commented "Sir Joseph stands in the ranks of Imperial statesmanship that include the illustrious Wolsly (sic), Chatham, Pitt and which have been expanded and adorned in later years by Rhodes, Borden, Laurier, Barton, Seddon, Kitchener, Botha, Hughes, Smuts and many others"[80]. News of his engagements must have been welcome relief in the newspaper amid the war reports and frequent casualty lists of local personnel.

In the meantime the tide of battle in Europe and Palestine had unexpectedly turned in favour of the allies. The Sentinel reported that the British had taken Neuve Chapelle and were making a great advance on the Somme Front. A few days later under the heading 'Allenby Strikes Again' the newspaper reported that the main Turkish army was in flight in Palestine and that a whole enemy regiment had been captured. The Australian Mounted Division played an important role in this action. The report further commented that General Allenby's troops were pressing north having taken 45,000 prisoners[81]. In France Australian troops captured Mount St.Quentin and Péronne at the expense of 3,000 casualties but this action marked a turning point in the upper Somme offensive. As a result Prime Minister Hughes paid a flying visit to France to congratulate his troops[82]. It began to look, at last, that there was light at the end of the tunnel and that victory was in sight.

Later that month in Palestine Allenby's troops annihilated the Turkish armies at Megiddo in what war historian Liddell-Hart described as 'one of the most quickly decisive campaigns and the most completely decisive battles in all history'[83]. To achieve the success Allenby was greatly assisted by aircraft and Emir Feisal's (later King Feisal) Arabs under Colonel T.E.Lawrence (Lawrence of Arabia) who had long been harassing, immobilising and demoralising the Turks with their guerilla type tactics. Also by the beginning of October in France the allies' battle front had extended and Field Marshall Sir Douglas Haig's troops had crossed the Hindenburg Line[84]. The Sentinel on 5th October 1918 announced that German troops were abandoning their positions on the Flanders coast and that Prince Max of Baden had sent a note to America's President Wilson, on behalf of the German Government, requesting him to "take up the question of bringing about peace".

Meanwhile Cook had been busily engaged visiting some of the British dockyards and Australian army units in the south of England and had also visited the Western Front. Together with writer Sir Arthur Conan Doyle, Australian war historian C.E.W.Bean, Sunday Times editor W.R.Berry and his attaché, Commander Latham, Cook visited frontal positions near Bellecourt. Returning to England he addressed members of the North Staffordshire Trades and Labour Council on 3rd October on the subject of 'war and industrial reconstruction' and recalled his visit to the battlefields of France. He said that he had been within 300 yds. of the Hindenburg Line. When he saw it "Australian troops had just gone through and were fighting for their lives on the other side". He also explained that he and Sir Arthur mounted an old tank in order to obtain a better view and narrowly missed being hit by a shell from a British howitzer! He told the Council that he had seen many sights which had impressed him and came away with the feeling more than ever settled in his mind that "if there be a sense of justice anywhere then someone ought to be punished for beginning this tragedy. It is of no use talking about a clean peace. There can only be one clean peace and that is after the culprits have been punished as they deserve"[85].

Early in November the Kaiser abdicated and social democrat, Friedrich Ebert, became Chancellor in time to accept the armistice terms offered by France's Marshall Foch on behalf of the victorious allies[86]. At 11 a.m. on 11th November hostilities ceased. The carnage was at last over. When the news was announced church bells tolled, flags were unfurled and people took to the streets in a series of victory celebrations.

4.   The Peace Makers

The Australian contribution to the war effort was not inconsiderable. The 1st Anzac Corps had distinguished itself in the bitter Somme offensive of 1914, the 2nd Corps at Ypres and Passchendaele. Other French place names were synonymous with Australian valour – Bullecourt, Villers-Bretonneux, Mont St.Quentin and Péronne, not to mention the daring assaults on the Hindenburg line. Not only did her sons and daughters serve with distinction in France and Palestine. The presence of the Australian Flying Corps in Mesopotania and her nurses in Salonica further contributed to the victory as did her navy on the high seas. It should also not be overlooked that Australia provided 6,000 personnel to work in the war factories in England[87].

Of the 417,000 men and women who voluntarily enlisted in the Australian forces, 330,000 served overseas. Of these two thirds became casualties and nearly 60,000 died. This was the highest casualty rate of any Empire force[88]. The cost of the war to Australia was assessed at £364 million pounds[89].

The armistice brought new responsibilities for Hughes and Cook as they were cabled to act on the Commonwealth's behalf at the peace negotiations. There was, in fact, talk of bad feeling between the two men and the Government was anxious that their opponents, Labor in particular, did not make political capital out of the matter. A London correspondent had written in Sydney's Daily Telegraph of "Mr.Hughes' contemptuous treatment of Sir Joseph" and that the latter "had been kept in complete ignorance of Mr.Hughes' plans, engagements and movements, his only source of information as to these matters being announcements in the London newspapers". Apparently the two men had not appeared on the same platform or visited the same place together for several months. The correspondent explained that although the strained relationship was not a secret Cook "did not desire publication of it, not, at least, before he returned to Australia and consulted his party". The report further explained that "the estrangement was primarily due to Mr.Hughes' jealous determination that Sir Joseph Cook should not share in his glory as a popular idol, set up by the Northcliffe press". The two eventually became reconciled and cabled the Australian Cabinet denying that there was any such disagreement and the debate was talked out[90].

The peace conference commenced at Versailles on 18th January 1919 with President Wilson's proposals providing the basis for discussion. Briefly the proposals called for the creation of a League of Nations, decolonisation, the right of all peoples to self-determination and free movement of goods and people[91]. Hughes was ready to accept the concept of a League of Nations but bitterly opposed a proposal to hand over the German colonies in the South West Pacific to be administered under a mandate that would permit freedom of migration. Under such provisions he realised that the Japanese would be able to migrate to New Guinea. He fought vigorously for Australia's right to annex the colonies maintaining that they were essential to Australian security. Hughes told the conference, and President Wilson in particular, that New Guinea was only 80 miles from Australia and that they did not really understand the problem[92].

Eventually he reluctantly agreed to accept a League of Nations mandate over the islands when it was conceded that Australian law, particularly that relating to trade and immigration, would prevail. He also argued strongly for a large war indemnity, demanding that the Germans pay towards the £364 million that Australia had spent on the war. However he eventually had to settle for half. Nevertheless Australian interests were ably defended at Versailles and she fared well as a result of, to quote Professor Frank Crowley, Hughes "shrewd belligerence"[93].

In addition to supporting Hughes in all aspects at the conference, Cook was also in favour of Germany losing all her overseas colonies and certain territory in Europe, particularly that of strategic value such as the Kiel canal[94]. He still shared the view expressed in his earlier speeches in England that Germany should be punished, but he appreciated that the allies could not inflict savage punishment on her. Whilst not particularly favouring leniency, he could not support vindictive or barbarous policies. David Lloyd George in his account of the peace conference stated that "Cook was amongst those fervent believers in the desirability and feasibility of a League of Nations". Hughes, however, according to Lloyd George was amongst those who "did not disguise their opinion that the League was doomed to disappoint the hopes of its devotees". Lloyd George regarded Hughes as 'cynical and outspoken'[95].

Hughes and Cook formed part of the British Empire delegation to the peace conference. As second Australian representative, however, it was not Cook's function to take the lead in any discussions at delegation meetings but that of Hughes. Cook's role was confined to answering questions or an occasional short statement, if the occasion so demanded. Equally, when the main peace conference was in session discussing any subject of concern to Australia it was Hughes' responsibility to speak, Cook being a mere observer. Nevertheless his conduct gained him the reputation of a valuable colleague and Lloyd George described him as "a man of calm and balanced judgement"[96].

One of the functions of the peace conference was to revise the national boundaries of Europe and few people perhaps realise that Cook was one of the architects responsible for the construction of the new nation of Czechoslovakia. In February he was invited to join the Committee which was appointed to define the borders of that nation. It is fair comment to say that, at the time, Cook knew little, if anything, about Czechoslovakia but he took heed of advice from experienced colleagues in particular Harold Nicholson of the Foreign Office and Sir Eyre Crowe. Nicholson in his account of the peace making described Cook as 'a nice sensible man and an angel of obedience'[97].

Notwithstanding such remarks, Cook had a mind of his own and was determined that the findings of the Committee would not result in a weak new state and a stronger Germany. The effect of his determination was the enlargement of the new state which was opposed by his colleagues from the British Empire delegation, but which was supported by the French.

Nicholson relates that during one session the French started an argument about the Delbrück nationality laws. When Cook was asked for his opinion he replied "Damn Delbrück!" To this Nicholson commented 'how right, how true' but further notes that such type of remark resulted in Cook being a thorn in the flesh of the Committee's interpreter whose face, on such occasion, would display an expression of acute agony twitches![98]. Despite differences of opinion the meetings of the Czechoslovak Committee were harmonious on the whole and it worked expeditiously to reach its conclusions. The first meeting was held on 27th February and its final report was approved by the co-ordinating body on 25th March[99].

Hughes and Cook temporarily returned to London for an Anzac parade which was to mark the first of many. This took place on 25th April. Australian war veterans, including many who had taken part in the Gallipolli landings, marched down the Strand led by their leader, Sir John Monash. His Royal Highness, the Prince of Wales, took the salute at Australia House and the aerobatics of the Australian Flying Corps overhead 'shook the soot from London's chimney pots' according to one newspaper. The whole event was a tremendous success[100].

The signing of the peace treaty took place on 28th June 1919 in the famous Hall of Mirrors at the Palace of Versailles. As official delegates to the conference, both Hughes and Cook were signatories to the peace document. After the ceremony the two made immediate plans to return to Australia. On the day they were due to leave England, Staffordshire's Sentinel newspaper printed a letter from Cook to H.Barrett Green, the editor, written at the Savoy Hotel, London on 6th July in which he said -

"It has been specially good and agreeable to see the old places once more and to renew the acquaintances and revive the memories of early days.

I am going back with a mind laden with glad and grateful memories and with a warmer place than ever in my heart for the great hearted people of the Potteries district"[101].

Hughes and Cook arrived in Freemantle, Western Australia on 24th August where Cook took much interest in the railway station which had been named after him[102]. They then travelled by means of the newly opened transcontinental railway reaching Melbourne on 31st August. The two were greeted with deafening cheers at the Spencer Street railway station. Someone put a diggers hat on Hughes' head and swathed him in an Australian ensign and the crowds shouted 'Little Digger' and 'You Beauty'. Some wept for joy in that moment of victory and achievement[103]. Cook subsequently returned home to Summer Hill, Sydney to be reunited with Mary and his children.

5. Treasurer

The following month, on 10th September 1919, Prime Minister Hughes rose to his feet in the House of Representatives and moved the ratification of the Treaty of Versailles. Speaking with emotion Hughes told the House - "we must turn now from war to peace. We live in a new world, a world bled white by the cruel wounds of war. Victory is ours, but the price of victory is heavy. The whole earth has been shaken to its very core. Upon the foundations of victory we would build the new temple of our choice"[104]. The motion was carried without dissent in both houses.

The mammoth task of organising the repatriation of the 270,000 Australian troops, many of them wounded, was already in hand. It had become apparent both to Hughes and Cook, when in Europe, that it would be necessary for a Minister to go to London to co-ordinate the demobilisation. The responsibility was to fall on the shoulders of Defence Secretary George Pearce who was despatched to London, arriving there as the Versailles Peace Conference was in its final stages. Due to the pressure applied by Pearce on British Government officials to provide the necessary shipping virtually all the troops were home by the end of December. This resulted in the shortening of the period of demobilisation by some months and a consequent saving of hundreds of thousands of pounds to Australia[105].

With Hughes' current popularity with the public, the Cabinet decided to capitalise on the situation and called an election for 13th December. The Nationalists defended their war record but also advocated increased independence for Australia in world affairs. Hughes, in a policy speech at Bendigo on 30th October, undertook to combat inflation, profiteering and industrial unrest, which he regarded as inter-related. Amongst other things he recommended a referendum with a view to amending the constitutional system which would result in the Commonwealth Government being granted the widest powers to regulate commerce, industry and employment and to nationalise monopolies[106].

Labor, under Frank Tudor, promised an extension of social services, increased age and invalid pensions and a national health service. The election was a three cornered fight due to the emergence of the Country Party, composed generally of farmers or farmers' union candidates who advocated increased subsidies, a reduction or abolition of tariff duties on agricultural implements, the encouragement of co-operative marketing and less government interference in trade and commerce generally.

The election resulted in the Nationalists winning all seats in the Senate with the exception of one. However in the House of Representatives they held 35 seats, with Labor 26, the Country Party 10, and 4 Independents. Cook secured an easy victory at Parramatta with a majority of almost 17,000[107]. He retained his position as Deputy Leader and Minister for the Navy while Hughes remained as Prime Minister and Attorney-General.

The election results meant that the Nationalists did not have a safe working majority in the House of Representatives. Furthermore although the Country Party, in general, preferred the Nationalists to Labor, its members were divided amongst themselves on many issues. For example, the Country Party though cautious about free trade in general was only committed to protectionism in certain limited areas. As a consequence, they could not always be relied upon to give the Government the necessary support. Hughes and Cook who had both been Freetraders before the war were now in the post-war world Protectionists[108]. To further complicate matters, the Nationalists included a group which was opposed to Hughes' leadership and this meant that the Government could be defeated on certain issues. The Whips had to be constantly on their toes!

In July 1920 Cook succeeded W.A.Watt as Treasurer, the latter having resigned from the Government following a disagreement with Hughes. Cook assumed office at a very difficult period: the height of the post-war boom. The Government was concerned about the debt and high inflation. His first budget was delivered on 16th September 1920. Briefly the measures provided for the early liquidation of the war debt and a reduction in government borrowing. The responsibility for banknote issue was transferred to the Commonwealth Bank whilst there were increases in postal charges, beer and tobacco duties and an increase of 5% on income tax. The provision of £3m to provide additional merchant shipping, which was designed to help the export trade, absorbed any surplus carried forward. The budget was not deflationary enough for the Opposition parties who unsuccessfully sought further economies[109].

His second budget was delivered on 29th September 1921 in a period of worldwide slump, after the post-war boom had come to an end. Continuing a deflationary policy he presented a 'stand still' budget granting slight concessions in income tax whilst using up reserves on recurrent spending. The Opposition parties were neither united nor clear as to alternative policies and were lacking particularly in suggestions as to how departmental expenditure could be reduced[110].

Critics of Cook's performance as Treasurer are agreed that whilst there were grounds for the deflationary policies of the first budget by reason of the inflation, there were not in the case of the second arising as it did out of a worldwide slump. They considered that then he should have grasped the opportunity to provide new public works and encourage the development of the country's natural resources. It is perhaps fair comment that any person who is responsible for Government finance, or even that relating to local authorities, is always an easy target for critics. Cook's term of office was during a particularly difficult economic period and it should also be noted that, at that time, the Government did not have the constitutional power to deal with Australia's finances effectively on a national scale. Cook never claimed to be anything more than an adequate Treasurer, admitting that he was no expert in financial matters[111]. He saw his task as performing a necessary unpleasant duty in the national interest. Cook was probably able to accept criticism more than most, but occasionally it would hurt.

Between April and September 1921 Cook was Acting Prime Minister due to Hughes attendance at the Imperial Conference in London. In Hughes' absence, Cabinet and party meetings became more harmonious than of late. The Prime Minister had began to alienate members of his Government and party by his overbearing pride and arrogance. As time went on he became careless in concealing his contempt for certain other members of his Cabinet[112]. In contrast to Hughes, Cook was more tactful with his colleagues and subordinates and allowed more freedom of discussion in meetings[113].

Sir Joseph and Lady Cook were extremely concerned about the after-care of the disabled ex-service personnel, showing much interest and giving encouragement to the various industries which had been established for them, for example the Disabled Soldiers

70

Weaving Industry, the Blinded Soldiers Tea Company as well as several others. On 23rd May in his capacity as Acting Prime Minister, Cook accompanied by his wife, took much pleasure in opening a Red Cross Exhibition at Sydney Town Hall which, according to Sydney's <u>Daily Telegraph</u> gave 'a splendid idea of what the Red Cross Society is doing in New South Wales for the after-care of disabled returned soldiers and the widows and dependents of fallen men'. Sir Joseph paid tribute to the magnificent work being done by the Society and to that done during the great war, the report also describing Lady Cook as 'a pillar of the Red Cross'[114].

In the meantime Cook had begun to show interest in succeeding Andrew Fisher as High Commissioner in London. Cook had strong opinions about the need for imperial co-operation to assist post-war reconstruction, believing that Australia's progress depended upon British investment, increased trade, expanded immigration and the security provided by imperial defence. As a consequence he was convinced that he would be of more use to Australia as High Commissioner than as Hughes' deputy[115]. No doubt Cook was also mindful of Hughes' attitude to him and his colleagues.

Shortly before Hughes' return, the Country Party, under Dr. Earle Page, made plans to defeat the Government and force his resignation. Page was confident that, with the voting support of the Labor members and those Nationalists who were opposed to Hughes' leadership, this could be achieved. Not long after Hughes' return Page, in the House of Representatives, moved a budget amendment and for some time it seemed doubtful whether the Government would survive. In the interim Cook's appointment as High Commissioner had been decided upon but the Cabinet did not announce it due to the crucial voting situation. Cook himself held out little hope of a successful division but due to the vigorous efforts of the Whips the Government survived Page's motion by 33 votes to 32.

At that time, when the fate of the Government hung in the balance, Cook sat in the Ministers' room in the House of Representatives talking to Senator George Pearce, the Defence Secretary. According to Pearce in his autobiography, Cook looked very miserable, and took rather a gloomy view of their prospects ("he being a good judge of a Parliamentary crisis"). Pearce explained that Hughes appeared with a grim smile on his face and began to sing the old song -

> "I'm coming, I'm coming
> And I know I soon shall go,
> I hear their gentle voices calling,
> Poor old Joe!"

Hughes then explained that he had received word from the Chief Whip that the 'numbers were right'[116]. Hughes, in fact, subsequently granted some budgetary concessions to Page, and was thus able to consolidate the security of the Government.

Cook resigned from the Government and Parliament on 11th November 1921[117] to enable him to take up the appointment of High Commissioner. He had been a Member of Parliament for over 30 years. A farewell luncheon was given for him and Lady Cook at Sydney Town Hall on 29th November[118]. In the meantime the Cooks made the necessary preparations for their long voyage and in early December they left for London with their two youngest children, Raymond and Connie.

XV XVI   Sir Joseph and Lady Cook shared in representing Australia in the imperial capital during the years of Sir Joseph's High Commissionership (1922-7) when Lady Cook proved an able and welcoming hostess. By this date her services to Australian life had been recognised by the award of the DBE.

Notes

1   G.Sawer. op.cit. p.113

2   N.Meaney. op.cit. p.261

3   Ibid p.260

4   Ferguson to Secretary of State for the Colonies, 24 Oct. 1918 (quoted by J.Murdoch. op.cit. p.250)

5   M.H.Ellis. op.cit. p.22

6   Ibid p.22

7   M.Clark. A short history of Australia (revised) 1981. p.199. (see also G.Sawer. op.cit. p.122)

8   G.Greenwood. op.cit. pp.231/2 (see also article by J.Prior in Sydney Sun 16 Aug. 1978)

9   M.Clark. op.cit. p.199

10   Liddell Hart. History of the World War 1914-18. 1970 p.47

11   Ibid p.50

12   Ibid p.50

13   Ibid p.49

14   F.Crowley. op.cit. p.312

15   Melbourne Argus, 4 Aug. 1914

16   Ibid 1 Aug. 1914

17   G.Greenwood. op.cit. p.261

18   Quoted by J.Murdoch. op.cit. p.288

19   N.Meaney. op.cit. p.174

20   J.Murdoch. op.cit. p.420

21   F.Crowley. op.cit. p.314

22   G.Sawer. op.cit. p.113

23   Ibid p.115

24   J.Murdoch. op.cit. p.290

25   Ex. info. G.Sawer

26   Ex. info. Mrs.M.Wood

27   Quoted by J.Murdoch. op.cit. p.277

28   F.Crowley. op.cit. p.318

29   Quoted by J.Murdoch. op.cit. p.298

30   Address to NSW Liberal Association 6th July 1915
      ('The Fighting Line' p.10).

31   Ibid

32   F.Crowley. op.cit. p.329

33   Conscription was introduced by Prime Minister
      Asquith in January 1916

34   Commonwealth Parliamentary Debates 79:7768 (10th
      May 1916)

35   M.Clark. op.cit. p.206

36   J.Murdoch. op.cit. p.318

37   Quoted by J.Murdoch. op.cit. p.316

38   G.Sawer. op.cit. p.134

39   Ex. info. A.Bebbington (see also A history of the
      World War 1914-18. Liddell Hart 1970. p.415)

40   Ex. info. Mrs.D.Holroyde

41   - ditto -

42   Ex. info. The Curator, Staffs. Regiment Museum

43   J.Murdoch. op.cit. p.334

44   G.Sawer. op.cit. p.156

45   Ibid pp.157/8

46   J.Murdoch. op.cit. p.420

47   Ibid p.339

48   Ex. info. G.Sawer

49   C.Hartley Gratton The South West Pacific since
      1900. University of Michigan Press 1963. p.54

50   M.H.Ellis. _op.cit._ p.22

51   _Ibid_ p.22

52   M.Clark. _op.cit._ p.207

53   _Ibid_ p.207

54   Quoted by G.Greenwood. _op.cit._ p.275

55   G.Sawer. _op.cit._ p.160

56   J.Murdoch. _op.cit._ p.343

57   24th September 1917 edition quoted by J.Murdoch. _op.cit._ p.344

58   G.Sawer. _op.cit._ p.176

59   _Sentinel_ 15th June 1918

60   _Ibid_

61   _Ibid_ 25th June 1918

62   _Ibid_ 27th June 1918

63   _The Times_ 29th June 1918

64   _Sentinel_ 12th July 1918

65   _Ibid_ 10th August 1918

66   Ex. info. Mrs.M.Wood (see _Sentinel_ for report of investiture 26th September 1918)

67   _Weekly Sentinel_ 20th July 1918

68   _Ibid_ 3rd August 1918

69   Cox _Potteries Annual & Year Book 1923_ (see also _Sentinel_ 9th November 1922)

70   _Sentinel_ 5th September 1918

71   The school log books record the event

72   _Sentinel_ 5th September 1918

73   Shenton had died the previous year but prior to that they had corresponded regularly

74   Ex info. Mesdames Weaver & Kelsall

75   Sentinel 5th September 1918

      Artistes at the concert included the Silverdale
      Glee Club (T.Mollineux, F.Washington, A.Shenton &
      J.Mollineux) and organist D.Brindley.

76   J.Murdoch's thesis incorrectly states that
      Wolstanton UDC conferred such honour (p.353). In
      fact at the luncheon given in Cook's honour by
      that Authority on 4th September 1918 the Chairman
      in his speech regretted that they could not offer
      him (i.e. Cook) the freedom of the district as
      they did not have the necessary power (Sentinel
      5th September 1918)

77   Newcastle-under-Lyme Borough Council records

78   Sentinel 6th September 1918

79   Ibid 16th September 1918

80   Ibid 13th September 1918

81   Ibid 22nd September 1918

82   F.Crowley. op.cit. p.351 (see also Liddell-Hart.
      op.cit. p.550)

83   Liddell-Hart. op.cit. p.553

84   Sentinel 4th October 1918

85   Ibid

86   Ibid 9th November 1918

87   C.H.Gratton. op.cit. p.47

88   F.Crowley. op.cit. p.348

89   M.Clark. op.cit. p.188

90   Daily Telegraph (Sydney) 10 December 1918 (see
      also G.Sawer. op.cit. p.177)

91   F.Crowley. op.cit. p.351

92   D.Lloyd George Memoirs of the Peace Conference
      1939 p.121

93   F.Crowley. op.cit. p.351

94   J.Murdoch. op.cit. p.371

95   D.Lloyd George. op.cit. p.423

96   Ibid p.421

97   H.Nicholson Peacemaking 1919. 1964. p.274

98   Ibid p.280

99   Ibid pp.272 & 289

100   G.F.Pearce Carpenter to Cabinet. 1951. p.152

101   Sentinel 8th July 1918

102   Daily Telegraph (Sydney) 28th August 1919

103   M.Clark. op.cit. p.189

104   Commonwealth Parliamentary Debates - 10th
       September 1919 (Ref.89. 12179)

105   G.F.Pearce. op.cit. pp.149/150

106   G.Sawer. op.cit. p.184

107   J.Murdoch. op.cit. p.421

108   G.Sawer. op.cit. p.201

109   Ibid p.205

110   ditto

111   Commonwealth Parliamentary Debates - 30th
       September 1920 (Ref.93.5211)

112   M.Clark. op.cit. p.193

113   J.Murdoch. op.cit. p.393

114   Daily Telegraph (Sydney) 24th May 1921

115   J.Murdoch. op.cit. p.379

116   G.F.Pearce. op.cit. p.155

117   G.Sawer. op.cit. p.189

118   Ex. info. J.Riley (who kindly furnished the writer
       with a copy of the menu)

... ine Pacific ... a cheap .
English-speaking peoples .. its munication. nere is nothing to prevent
potent, magnetic sway. Asked whether newspaper syndicates from having each
he liked the work, Mr. Cook said he day a letter from some noted pressman
did, immensely. " Whether my position containing a *resumé* of the previous

THE HON. A. J. THYNNE, M.L.C. THE HON. JOSEPH COOK, M.P. THE HON. J. GAVAN-DUFFY. M.P.
JAMES DALGARNO, SECRETARY TO THE CONFERENCE. THE HON. J. A. COCKBURN, M.P. THE HON. W. P. REEVES.

in the Cabinet does or does not help day's events, instead of the brief, scrappy
labor is for others to say. My aim, at cablegrams that frequently contradict
any rate, is to show that the demands of each other, so fragmentary are the words
¹s have a more solid basis of reason from which a connected statement has
·erall·· ·od ·nd ·¹ · he ···¹¹ A ·o··

XVII   Joseph Cook, as Postmaster General of New South Wales,
chairing the Postal and Telegraphic Conference of 1896 which
nominated two delegates from Australia to attend the Pacific
Cable Commission which was soon to meet in England and
recommend linking Vancouver by cable with Australia.

XVIII   A group of Australian politicians taken at Parliament House in 1914 with Earl Grey sitting next to Sir Joseph Cook as Prime Minister in the front row. Seated on the extreme left is Andrew Fisher who succeeded Cook later that year.

XIX   Sir Joseph Cook surveying one of the War Bonds succesfully launched to support the War effort : as Prime Minister he sold the first War Bond personally.

XX   Sir Joseph Cook (second from the right on the back row) with Lloyd
George and other dominion representatives at the Peace Conference after
the First World War.'Billy'Hughes, Australian Prime Minister, is seated
third from the right on Lloyd George's immediate left.

XXI   Cook addressing troops in South Australia as they prepared for
service in the First World War. The figure with the hat to the immediate
rear of Cook is William Hughes, then Prime Minister of Australia.

XXII   Cook as Prime Minister was pleased to welcome the battle
cruiser "Australia" and other vessels under the command of
Admiral Patey to Australian waters on the formation of this
independent force which as Defence Minister he had sought to
create.

AUSTRALIA DAY.

PRINCE OF WALES
AT
COMMISSIONER'S RECEPTION.

The greatest and perhaps the most brilliant reception ever given in connection with the celebration of Australia Day took place late yesterday evening in Australia House. The building possesses one of the most magnificent interiors in London, and yesterday it was further beautified by banks of flowers and palms. The cinema hall, where daily the attractions of the Dominion are shown on the screen, was transformed into a ball-room. Sir Joseph and Lady Cook received their guests in the library, and the Exhibition Hall, the marble-covered floor and walls and fine pillars of which are among the sights that few visitors to the metropolis miss, was utilised as a supper-room, where the 1,500 guests could "listen-in" to the Australian concert, which was shared by many thousands more throughout the country.

The Prince of Wales, who was attended by Captain the Hon. Piers Legh, arrived before ten o'clock, and was given an enthusiastic welcome by the crowd which had assembled outside the building. His greeting by the great gathering was equally cordial. Many of the guests were presented to him by his host and hostess, and with not a few of them he exchanged remarks which showed how vivid and pleasant were his recollections of his journeys in the Commonwealth.

His Royal Highness had travelled from Wiltshire specially to attend the reception, and on his arrival at Australia House was reminded, on noticing the street vendors that he was not wearing the wattle. He purchased a sprig just before entering and placed it in his buttonhole. During his tour of the building he visited the ball room and danced with Miss _____ the wife of the High Commissioner.

A novel and noteworthy feature of the celebration was that for the first time in history, the High Commissioner of Australia, Sir Joseph Cook, was enabled to address an audience scattered throughout practically the whole of the United Kingdom and no mean part of the Continent of Europe, and put before his hearers in most cases comfortably seated at their own firesides, what Australia means to its children and what they hope it may yet be.

For broadcasting people it was an "All-Australia" evening. Just after tea Dame Nellie Melba talked to the children by wireless. At eight o'clock, before an excellent concert of Australian music was entered upon, Sir Joseph Cook broadcasted the following speech:

To-day is our birthday. We are 135 years old to-day. Australia will celebrate it as a holiday. And there will be pilgrimages to Kurnell, the spot on the shores of Botany Bay where Captain Cook and his comrades first landed on the soil of our radiant and happy land. Hundreds of thousands of our children, and grown ups too, will sing "Advance, Australia Fair," followed by the National Anthem. In this way they will think of their country as inseparably associated with their king. And their thoughts will flow in gratitude to the Motherland who gave them this great new land in which they dwell, and who through all these years has protected and nurtured them while they pioneered and developed the last and best and brightest of the continents of the world. And as they think of their privileges there will be a generous desire to share them with the _____ overcrowded Motherland.

Last year 25,000 migrants left these shores for the New Britain in the Pacific, to be followed as the years come and go by multitudes more. They will go out not to a foreign country but to live on the Australian section of the great Imperial estate. There they will speak the same language, read the same history, inherit the same glorious traditions, sing the same songs, salute the same flag, enjoy the same faith and freedom. At present our national life and institutions are in their springtime. Our hopes are high and our enterprises eager. Our faces are to the rising sun.

To-day we are broadcasting to the world our high hopes and aspirations, and there will follow immediately some tuneful and happy glimpses of the spirit already stirring within us. One day, and that soon, we shall as surely broadcast the story of the development of a national life richer and rarer and more wonderful than anything that has gone before. Our one unfaltering purpose is to make Australia a newer and greater Britain in a newer and greater _____

THE GUESTS

Among those invited to be present were:

The Archbishop of Canterbury and Mrs. Randall Davidson, the Duke and Duchess of Devonshire, the Duke and Duchess of Marlborough, the Duke and Duchess of Portland, the Duke and Duchess of Sutherland, the Marchioness of Aberdeen and Temair, the Marquis and Marchioness of Bath.

The Earl of Balfour, Admiral of the Fleet Earl Beatty, Field Marshal Earl Haig, the Earl and Countess of Harrowby, the Earl and Countess of Darnley, the Earl and Countess of O _____

XXIII   Sir Joseph Cooks Australia Day Broadcast, January 1923.

IV   High Commissioner and Retirement

1.   High Commissioner

Except for a boisterous time in the Mediterranean the voyage was uneventful and the Cook family arrived in Plymouth on the P & O liner 'Mantua' on 13th January 1922[1].   There the vessel was boarded by M.L.Shepherd, the Acting High Commissioner, who travelled with them to London where they arrived two days later.   The capital was shrouded in dense fog on their arrival and the streets overlaid with snow which Raymond and Connie had not seen before[2].

At a press conference Cook observed that although the cost of the passage between Australia and England had more than doubled since he emigrated, it was a striking fact that the science of ocean travelling had not shortened the distance by a single day!   He commented on the need for the speeding up of communications between the two countries and of the interest shown in Australia of the possibility of communicating by airship.   He then paid tribute to Frank Tudor, leader of the Australian Federal Labor Party, of whose death he had just learned - 'although in opposite camps for 21 years we have never forfeited our mutual respect and all our personal relations were most pleasant and intimate'[3].

Subsequently he went on to say that

"After more than 30 uninterrupted and strenuous years of public service I am changing over to do duty on another part of the same great Imperial family estate. It may be that on some matters connected with the management of this estate we have differing points of view.   Looking at things from another angle we may get a slightly different focus but the final objectives are the same"[4].

Asked about opportunities in Australia for emigrants he replied 'please do not use that word, they are migrants from one part of the Empire to another. Australia has spent £30m repatriating service men and settling them, not to mention millions also spent on new housing etc.   Australia is still suffering from the result of the war but we are making a recovery, to say the least, as rapid and permanent as that in any other section of the globe.   The prospects are excellent, the harvests good and the secondary industries are, on the whole, healthy, vigorous and sound'[5].

As he had explained at the press conference, Cook had, in effect, switched careers.   He was no longer an elected representative of the people but an appointed public servant. As such, his primary function as High Commissioner was to act as Australia's spokesman on policies which affected Britain. Furthermore he was now also Australia's diplomatic representative to the League of Nations and to any international conferences held in Europe. He was also required to represent Australia at all important social functions in Britain.

From the moment of his arrival in Britain, Cook devoted himself to the promotion of his Government's policies[6]. He extolled the virtues of Australia and sought to encourage trade between the two countries. He also endeavoured to encourage the investment of British capital in Australia. Enthusiastically promoting immigration schemes, he commended Australia as 'the land of promise' or 'the land of better chance'[7]. He was hopeful that Australia's immigration proposals would 'lead thousands of men unable to secure employment here to go out to the great open spaces of the Australian countryside and become useful citizens'[8]. Cook developed new promotional methods and his enthusiasm resulted in far more comprehensive publicity schemes for Australia than had been the case under his predecessors. More money was spent on advertising and regular exhibitions and film shows were introduced at Australia House which attracted thousands[9]. He also broadcast on the radio on the subject of opportunities in Australia.

The formal occasions on which Cook attended as his country's representative gave him immense pleasure, be it at Australia House, or elsewhere. From past experience he carried himself with the utmost propriety and decorum in a dignified manner which gave him credit. One of the first major functions he attended as Australia's representative was the marriage of HRH Princess Mary and Viscount Lascelles at Westminster Abbey on 28th February 1922[10]. He also loved the pomp and ceremony of such annual events as the State Opening of Parliament and the Lord Mayor of London's show. Likewise the Cooks regularly attended Buckingham Palace garden parties[11]. That the former pit boy from Silverdale should be accepted by the aristocracy of the Empire absolutely delighted him[12]. He also inspected factories where orders were in hand for the Australian Government checking on their progess.

Certain Government departments were represented at Australia House including Trade & Customs, Markets & Migration together with the Navy, Military & Air Force Boards. From a policy aspect their staff were directly responsible to their respective departments in Australia. However they remained answerable for their work and behaviour to Cook who was also responsible for all appointments to the Commission's staff. The most significant of the High Commissioner's functions at Australia House was therefore administration including control of expenditure. Upon assuming office Cook found that the administration of the Commission was not to his liking and, consequently, he began a major overhaul with a view to securing economy coincidental with increased efficiency. This was resented by certain departmental heads who strongly resisted Cook's efforts to impose any changes on them[13].

In January 1923 Sir Joseph and Lady Cook gave what one newspaper described as 'the greatest and perhaps the most brilliant reception in connection with the celebration of Australia Day'. The cinema at Australia House was transformed into a ballroom and the exhibition hall was utilised as a supper room, the Cooks receiving their guests in the library. There were 1,500 distinguished guests including HRH the Prince of Wales, the Duke & Duchess of Marlborough, the Duke & Duchess of Portland and the Duke & Duchess of Sutherland. A noteworthy feature of the celebration was that for the first time the High Commissioner was able to broadcast to practically the whole of the United Kingdom and a large part of Europe. At eight o'clock, prior to a concert of Australian music, Sir Joseph made his broadcast (Illustration XXIII). A friend of the Cooks, opera singer Dame Nellie Melba, was also featured in the celebrations[14].

Major social functions attended during that year included the marriage of HRH the Duke of York and Lady Elizabeth Bowes-Lyon at Westminster Abbey on 26th April and the assembly of the fleet at Spithead in November[15].

On the family front, the Cooks resided at 36 Queens Gate in the south west of London during the period of Sir Joseph's term of office as High Commissioner. They regularly entertained relatives and friends there including Arthur Hassam and his family. Hassam, as it happened, was Mayor of Newcastle-under-Lyme at this period and Cook travelled north to share the occasion of the Mayor's Sunday and parade with his life long friend on 12th November 1922[16]. Dame Nellie Melba was also a regular visitor to the Cook residence, singing at their soirées. The Cook's son, Raymond, was a boarder at the Ley's School, Cambridge, a Methodist foundation, but his parents frequently visited him, staying at the University Arms nearby. Connie remained at home with her parents but attended a ladies college in London[17].

The following year, 1924, was a busy one for Sir Joseph and Lady Cook, not only from an official aspect, but from a family point of view. The British Empire

Exhibition was held on a 220 acre site at Wembley on the outskirts of London. Opened by His Majesty the King on April 23rd, its purpose was to display the resources and possibilities of every part of the Empire, and the Governments of nearly all the Dominions, Colonies and Dependencies lent their active support to the promoters. The exhibition had been projected as far back as 1913 and when it eventually materialised was on a scale of unprecedented grandeur. Cook, as High Commissioner, devoted a considerable amount of time and energy organising the Australian pavilion for which he received much praise. A book was published to coincide with the event to which Cook contributed the chapter on Australia[18].

By this time, the Cooks had been joined by their daughter, Winifred, who greatly assisted her parents in their duties, also proving to be very popular in the London social circles. Lady Cook did not particularly enjoy the diplomatic social life and attended certain functions more out of duty than by choice. This is not to infer, however, that Sir Joseph did not receive the full support of his wife. Lady Cook did her duty and worked extremely hard on her husband's behalf at all times. However, she preferred to remain in the background but this was not always possible as she fully appreciated. But if there was an occasion when Lady Cook was indisposed or felt unable to attend and Winifred was available, she would deputise[19]. One such occasion was on 20th May 1924 when she launched the Orient liner "Orama" at Vickers' shipyard, Barrow-in-Furness. At that time the 20,000 ton liner was the largest that had been built at that yard[20].

Winifred became engaged to fellow Australian Robert F.Cook M.C. (no relation!) and their London wedding on 19th November 1924 was a most popular event in the social calendar of that year. Music was especially composed for the occasion which took place at St.Clement Dane's Church in the Strand, following which there was a long hold up of traffic as the large number of distinguished guests streamed across the road from the church to Australia House for the reception. The High Commission had not been used for such an event previously and, at the reception which was held in the library, Australian wines were served[21].

In 1925 honour was conferred on Lady Cook. In the King's Birthday Honours List it was announced that she was to become a Dame of the Order of the British Empire "in recognition of her services in connection with visitors to London from the Commonwealth of Australia"[22]. The press acknowledged that Dame Mary had "worked hard since she came to London rendering invaluable service as wife of the High Commissioner and the honour is very highly deserved"[23].   Naturally the Cook family were very proud of the award.

Later that year, Her Majesty Queen Alexandra died and at her funeral service, held at Westminster Abbey on 27th November, Sir Joseph represented the Commonwealth[24].

On 25th April 1926 Arthur Hassam died suddenly after collapsing at his home at Newcastle-under-Lyme. He and Sir Joseph had been friends since they had worked together in the mines at Silverdale. They had both achieved success in their own individual spheres but remained in contact, despite Cook emigrating to Australia, by regularly corresponding with each other. Since Cook had returned to England in 1921 (and also during the period of his earlier visit in 1918/19) the two men had lost no opportunity in meeting each other. Hassam, a successful consultant mining engineer, had also achieved success in local politics and had been Mayor of Newcastle-under-Lyme on three occasions, 1922-25. A few days later Sir Joseph, with heavy heart, hurried north to the funeral of his late friend attending the service at St.George's Church, Newcastle-under-Lyme and the subsequent internment at Newcastle cemetery, before returning to London to fulfil other engagements[25].

The following year, 1927 saw the termination of Sir Joseph's term as High Commissioner. Prior to that, however, on 17th March, Dame Mary launched the warship HMAS Australia at John Brown's Clydebank shipyard[26]. To mark the event she was presented with a silver rose bowl which she treasured for many years[27].   Again, on a nautical front, on 31st May the Cooks witnessed, at the same yard, the launching of the 'Canberra' by HRH Princess Mary, Viscountess Lascelles[28].

In March it was announced that Sir Granville Ryrie had been appointed to succeed Cook as High Commissioner. Cook's official term of office expired on 11th May but he remained in office until his successor arrived in July. A valedictory dinner in honour of Sir Joseph and Dame Mary was given at the Savoy Hotel, London on 16th May by the Rt. Hon. L.S. Amery M.P., Secretary of State for Dominion Affairs and the Colonies.   On 19th July the Lord Mayor of London, Sir Rowland Blades, gave a similar function at the Mansion House. The latter was a most splendid occasion at which the band of HM Coldstream Guards played during dinner. Colonial and Dominion representatives were present together with many other distinguished guests and the names on the table plan read like extracts from the pages of 'Debrett'[29].

During his term of office Cook represented

Australia at a score or so of conferences[30]. He attended the Genoa Economic Conference in 1922 and also assemblies of the League of Nations Internal Labour Organisation at Geneva, but was required to do little more than attend and subsequently report to his Government. He also attended the general assemblies of the League of Nations but his main work was at the annual sessions of the Mandates Commission where he ably defended Australia's administration of the mandated territories of New Guinea and Nauru[31]. It was in Geneva that Cook made the acquaintance of author and social activist, Vera Brittain. By coincidence, Miss Brittain was born in Newcastle-under-Lyme quite near to the residence of Cook's now deceased friend, Arthur Hassam. In 1922 Miss Brittain went to Geneva to collect material for a commissioned magazine article and met Cook en route. She later heard him at the Mandates Commission 'wrathfully endeavouring to answer satisfactorily some awkward questions asked by the Commissioners on the subject of Nauru'[32]. Cook habitually addressed Miss Brittain as 'Little Newcastle'[33].

Cook's overhaul of the administration at Australia House resulted in the number of staff being reduced from 321 to 199 and annual running costs were reduced from £123,776 to £87,139[34]. During his period of office 250,000 migrants made their way to Australia from Great Britain. He calculated that the work of the High Commissioner had increased fourfold during his term of office and contended that it would increase further as the future of Australia realised its full potential. The increase in migrants was in no small way due to Cook's efforts in publicising the Commonwealth and he was also proud of the fact that he was responsible for raising £50m in new loans for Australia[35]. With his immense enthusiasm and energy, Cook represented his country well and proved an excellent High Commissioner.

On the morning of 10th August 1927 Cook attended a meeting of the Privy Council following which, at an audience with His Majesty the King, his appointment as High Commissioner was relinquished[36].

On 20th of that month Sir Joseph and Lady Cook, together with their son and daughter, Raymond and Connie, sailed from Tilbury for Australia on the liner 'Orsova'. On the dockside prior to their departure, their friend Dame Nellie Melba sang the Scottish song 'Will you no come back again' to them[37]. Sir Joseph thanked all who had made their stay in London so pleasurable. He said "I do not like leaving London behind me. I cannot understand the man who does" The Daily Telegraph commented that this quotation bore a Johnsonian stamp about it![38]. He continued -

"I have enjoyed every minute of my stay here and have found equal pleasure in my work.

One thing which has interested me has been to watch the behaviour of this old country towards all the troubles and trials of the post war period. Some difficulties still exist and one of the most difficult is the struggle against the barriers which your water tight departments and methods often create. The struggle is still going on despite all the efforts which were made at the recent International Economic Conference to arrest it. You have this strange anomoly before you that whilst the production of the world is increasing, the trade of the world is not increasing in the same proportion. That is the real trouble at the moment as far as I see it."

He liked the slogan of the British Market Board - "Buy where you sell - sell where you buy!"[39].

Another reporter commenting on the departure of the former High Commissioner wrote - "The secret of Sir Joseph is of course the secret of all our Empire builders, a combination of immense vigour, intense concentration, entire forgetfulness of self in the service of the State and a broad understanding of, and sympathy with, his fellow men"[40].

The tributes having been paid, the 'Orsova' bore the Cook family down the Thames towards the sea for their long voyage home.

2. "Silchester" & Retirement

The Cooks arrived in Western Australia on 20th September. Sir Joseph was said to be looking extremely well after the long voyage and he told reporters that 'it was good to see the friendly lights as the ship steamed into Fremantle in the early hours'. Lady Cook endorsed the sentiment by saying that she was quite excited at 'the nearness of reunion with old friends'.

At a civic reception given in his honour by the Mayor and Councillors, Sir Joseph in a speech, maintained that there was undoubtedly a better knowledge and appreciation of Australia in London than there had been 5 or 6 years previously. He outlined the progress made during his term of office and said that although 250,000 new migrants had made their way from Great Britain to Australia during such period he could have sent "half a dozen times as many ... The problem is not one of finding suitable migrants in London so much as of finding opportunities for them in Australia".

He told fruit growers that there was a great future for the Australian fruit trade in London but the growers must learn to supply what the London market required rather than what they thought the market ought to be satisfied with. In conclusion he said that Australia was now more prominently on the map although he appreciated that this was also due to the accumulated efforts of his predecessors. He urged his fellow countrymen "to do nothing that would tend to despoil the fair name of the finest country in the world in the eyes of Great Britain"[41].

Cook was now almost 67 years of age. He had long since reached the decision not to return to politics as he felt that to do so might result in failure. Consequently he purchased a large property on Trahlee Road at Bellevue Hill, an exclusive eastern suburb of Sydney, and named it "Silchester" after the two villages where he and his wife were born. From the irregular shaped house a magnificent view of Sydney Harbour and the north shore could be obtained, more so from the drawing room which was particularly noted for its panoramic views. The house was renowned for its interior woodwork, installed by the former owner, which was complemented by the high quality furniture purchased in London during Sir Joseph's term as High Commissioner. Other prized items of furniture were also in the house, including a writing table of Australian woods presented to Lady Cook by the women of Sydney. There were some fine examples of landscapes by English painters in the dining room and in other rooms there were many items of cut glass or silver which had been presented, on occasions, to Sir Joseph or Lady Cook. The master had his own den which was lined with well filled bookshelves!

Lady Cook was assisted in running the house by daughters Connie and Mrs.King (i.e. Annette, now widowed), together with a maid. Sir Joseph and Lady Cook, both of them keen gardeners, took pleasure in tending the large garden[42].

In the following year Cook was temporarily brought out of retirement. The South Australian State Government had sought financial aid from the Commonwealth Government on the ground that certain federal legislation had been the cause of a budgetary deficit. As a consequence, the Commonwealth Government decided to appoint a Royal Commission to look into the matter and Cook was invited to be Chairman, a post which he was delighted to accept. The Commission was requested not only to investigate the State Government's claim but also to give some guidance as to future financial relations between the Commonwealth and State Governments. The other members of the Commission were

H.Brookes, a prominent Melbourne businessman, and A.E.Barton, a Sydney accountant[43].

The report, published in April 1930, was a well ordered and clear document, which according to Brookes, owed much to Cook's pleasant, but forceful lead. The Commissioners, in fact, found that State Government policies had, to a certain extent, been responsible for the deficit. However they also found that certain federal laws (in particular, the tariff and the Conciliation & Arbitration Act) had tended to favour the industries of New South Wales and Victoria to the detriment of those of South Australia. Notwithstanding, they also found that certain federal action, such as the construction of the transcontinental railway and the locking of the River Murray had assisted the state. Taking all factors into consideration, the Commissioners found that federal legislation had tended to improvish South Australia. As a consequence they recommended, inter alia, that £1m be paid to the state, a recommendation which was accepted by the Federal Government. Cook and his colleagues, however, were unable to recommend any formula regarding future financial relationships between the Commonwealth and State Governments. Nevertheless the report became a small part of a general financial reassessment in which the Commonwealth Government became more disposed to grant money to poorer States[44].

That same month Cook participated in the first private telephone call between Great Britain and Australia but the occasion was not of his making. Cook's daughter, Winifred, then living at Bradford, learned that the service was to be introduced and, accordingly, booked a call. The result was that on 13th April she was able to speak to her surprised, but delighted, parents at their Sydney home. Also participating in the call was her husband and their five year old daughter Jocelyn whom Sir Joseph and Lady Cook had never seen and they were naturally overjoyed to speak to their granddaughter. Jocelyn, now Mrs.Fearnley, remembers the occasion well but naturally with being so young at the time, can recall little of the conversation! It is befitting that Sir Joseph should have participated in that telephone call because of his interest in telecommunications no doubt arising from his early service as Postmaster General. Whenever he arrived at a destination after a long voyage he always complained of the absence of news, other than that received at ports of call, and would remark of the need for improvement in communications[45].

In the 1930s Cook arranged for 'Silchester' to be demolished and for the site to be redeveloped, thereby securing additional investments for his retirement. A block of luxury flats was built on the site and the Cooks eventually resided in the one of their choice which, like their former house, enjoyed magnificent views of Sydney Harbour.

Sir Joseph's political career now ended, the couple lived quietly at their Bellevue Hill home. He took great pleasure in the increasing number of his descendants[46]. Although not politically active, Cook maintained an interest in politics and world affairs. He also maintained his interest in the church and continued to preach or speak at functions, though not so frequently as he had in the past.

Cook was 78 years of age at the outbreak of the Second World War. No doubt memories came flowing back to him of the fateful day when he was Prime Minister at the outbreak of the Great War. H.G.Wells had, in fact, referred to that event as "the war to end all wars ..... the last war". Regrettably this was not to be the case. Germany, under Adolf Hitler, rearmed in violation of the Versailles Treaty and in 1938 its forces occupied Austria. In March 1939 Hitler seized the Czechoslovakian capital, Prague, and on 1st September German troops invaded Poland. As a consequence Britain declared war on Germany and on 3rd September Australia entered the conflict. Prime Minister Robert Menzies in officially informing his fellow Australians of the situation concluded by saying - "May God in his mercy and compassion grant that the world may soon be delivered from this agony"[47].

In July 1940 Cook attended a 'Pleasant Sunday Afternoon Service' at the Lyceum Hall, Sydney. He told the congregation -

"We are at war and the only thing to do is to roll your sleeves up and see it through. The world needs England today more than ever before. She is like a rock in a ruined land.

Beware of those people who want to establish a new world order. A 'new order' often means something very old that has grown blue mouldy and has whiskers on it. People are told that if they only believe in the 'new order' all will be well. Don't you believe such nonsense. The old things of the world today are the wisest and best things I know.

Today there are Mussolini, Hitler and Stalin and I do not know how many other dictators. Do not introduce that sort of thing into our new Australia. The people who are being governed the best are those who have the system of election called 'First past the post'. That system has stood the test of time.

It is not an easy job to set the world right. Hitler is not going to do it and Mussolini or Stalin cannot do it because Almighty God has something to do with the disposition of the races of the world"[48].

This occasion appears to be Cook's final recorded public appearance.

Cook resisted pressure to compile his memoirs, even destroying many personal papers before his death[49]. Dame Mary never kept a diary and, likewise, she said that she would never write her memoirs[50]. Cook viewed his career with satisfaction, considering that he had always done his duty and never avoided responsibilities. He was satisfied that he had led a worthy and profitable life in the sight of God and man, and was immensely proud of having held the offices of Prime Minster and High Commissioner. He wrote in his diary that he was prepared to 'approach end of life with a fortitude quiet as earth's at the shedding of leaves'[51].

Although he loved his adopted country, he never lost a true affection for the village of his birth. He received the greatest pleasure from welcoming fellow Daliens who took the opportunity of calling on him when visiting the Commonwealth. He would discuss with them characters of the village and what changes had taken place since he left and what the place would be like in say another century. Cook would also recall his school days and his early years in the mines[52].

At the beginning of July 1947 Cook was taken ill at his Bellevue Hill home. He had been ill for about three weeks when he died on the afternoon of 30th July of a heart ailment[53]. He was 86 years of age. Ironically Sir Joseph had, for some time, been nursing his wife who sadly was becoming senile.

A state funeral was held on Friday 1st August commencing with a service at the Wesleyan Chapel, Castlereagh Street, Sydney. The service was conducted by Rev.G.E.Johnson, President of the New South Wales Conference of Methodist Churches in Australasia, assisted by Rev.R.B.Lew, Secretary of the Conference. The chapel was crowded to overflowing and the dense crowds which thronged the route of the funeral cortege were a striking tribute to the regard in which the veteran statesman was held by the community generally. The address was given by Rev.Wallace Deane, an old friend of the family who in paying tribute to the 'distinguished Methodist statesman' spoke of Cook's vigorous and logical style of public address -

"He always spoke like a man who had lived through all he said and thoroughly believed in the truth of his words ..... Irreproachable in conduct, slowly, but surely, he moved upwards in the estimation of his fellows, yet he never moved away from his religious convictions and moral conduct. The only gibe his opponents could level at him was his goodness of life ..... He had a certain beautiful humility of spirit which blended well with the natural dignity of his bearing. He was always dignified but he had no false pride ..... There is no doubt that Sir Joseph, being born in England, was a devoted and loyal Englishman. At the same time he was a truly great Australian whose patriotism shone like the meridian sun. He loved the land of the southern cross and lived for the welfare of the Empire, striving to make stronger and still stronger the bonds which bind us to the Mother Country. In this respect he is an example for every true Australian".[54]

The hymns included 'Day is dying in the west' and the aptly chosen 'Go labour on spend and be spent' which included the words -

'Toil on and in thy toil rejoice
For toil comes rest for exile home'[55]

Pallbearers included former Prime Minister, William Hughes, W.H.Kelly a survivor of Cook's ministry of 1913-14 and Senator Ashley (also representing the Commonwealth Government). The Governor-General and the Governor-General of New South Wales were represented at the funeral as were many Government Departments. Following the service the cortege immediately left for the Northern Suburbs Crematorium where Cook was cremated. Subsequently a simple commemorative plaque was erected there.

News of Cook's death was greeted with sadness in the area of his birth in England. At a meeting of Newcastle Borough Council on 30th July the Mayor, Alderman F.T.Brant, said that "it was with great regret that they heard of his death. They were all proud of the success that he had achieved". Members stood in tribute, following which they resolved to forward a letter of sympathy to Lady Cook[56].

In addition to his widow, Cook was survived by five sons and three daughters, a sixth son (John Hartley) having died a few years before. He left an estate valued at £23,269[57].

To commemorate Cook's death a play relating his story was broadcast from Radio 2UE Sydney on the day following his death[58]. I understand that this was privately recorded by the Cook family for the benefit of future generations. In 1972 his portrait was featured in a series of stamps commemorating former Prime Ministers of the Commonwealth[59]. Portraits of Sir Joseph Cook hang in Parliament House, Canberra and the National Gallery, Edinburgh respectively.

Dame Mary survived her husband by three years. When she died in 1950 a further commemorative plaque was placed adjacent to the one relating to her late husband.

Epilogue

Cook has largely been ignored by historians, possibly because of his early departure from the infant Australian Labor Party. Certainly in this respect he is regarded by some as a 'double' sinner. Possibly a further reason is that as he was most frequently in Opposition, and represented minority interests, there is a tendency to underestimate his abilities. His only notable Federal Parliamentary achievements were the Defence Act 1909 and the double dissolution of 1914. The former, however, was most important as it was responsible for the establishment of defence forces in Australia and Cook is regarded as the 'Father' of the Australian Navy. Even when in office Cook seems to have been one of those men destined to be a loyal second in command, following dutifully in the footsteps first of Reid in New South Wales, and then of Deakin and Hughes in the Federal Government. However he mastered the art of living with their individual temperaments during their respective terms of office. He was Prime Minister in his own right for only 14 months but he achieved the distinction of being in such office when Australia was drawn into the Great War. However, when assessing Cook's political career one should not overlook his performance as Postmaster General and Secretary for Mines and Agriculture in the New South Wales Legislative Assembly.

If there is any aspect of Cook's character which relatives feel has been misrepresented, or misunderstood, by historians, it is that of the man's sense of humour. He has been described as solemn and humourless, etc. For example Deakin's biographer J.A. La Nauze describes Cook as an 'irascible, untiring, humourless little man'[60]. J.Murdoch states that 'he grew up with a deficient sense of humour ..... he took his work so seriously it was only the members of his family who were able to observe fully that he had his lighthearted moments'[61]. Cook's relatives, in fact, maintain that he had a warm sense of humour. His grand-daughter, Mrs.M.Wood states that 'his smile was hard to see behind his moustache and beard but one had only to look at his blue eyes to see them smiling'. Concurring with this view, Malcolm Ellis in an article on Cook refers to his 'bright smiling eye' and his 'usual good humour'[62]. Cook's niece, Mrs.D.Holroyde, agrees that he was a quiet, serious minded person but that he did like a joke. According to family friend Rev.Wallace Deane, Cook told him that 'he had trained himself in every day life to say little but to listen intently for the information he needed'[63]. Sir Robert Garran, the first Solicitor General of the Commonwealth, liked and respected Cook very much but considered him 'fairly stiff and non-effusive in his official relations and parliamentary activities'[64]. Cook's image certainly did not go down well with some Australians who considered him to be straightlaced on account of him being both a preacher and a teetotaller. However in certain company Cook blossomed. Malcolm Ellis also confirms that Cook would be 'at home in any well bred company'[65]. Historians compare Cook with a generation of politicians who tended to be fruity and effusive in speech and mien - Deakin was known as 'Affable Alfred', Reid was known as 'Yes - No' because of his ambivalent attitude to Federation, while 'Billy' Hughes ranted and raved. By contrast Cook's steadiness and balanced judgement, whilst estimable qualities, provided less column inches for the journalists.

Being born at Silverdale at the time that he was, and sharing the experiences that he did, I feel that he would not have survived let alone have achieved the success that he did without a sense of humour. Humour is very localised, particularly in the Midlands and North of England, just as dialect is. North Staffordshire people, in general, have a keen sense of humour. It is, however, a dry sense of humour which may not be appreciated or may be misunderstood outside the area. What one thinks of another person's sense of humour must depend largely upon your own. However important a topic this may be to some people, this should not be allowed to detract from the great work that Cook did and also from the fact that he was a great parliamentarian. No one seems to dispute that. Deakin's biographer J.A. La Nauze, despite earlier remarks says of Cook - "his energy was undoubted, his parliamentary sense shrewd and his confidence in himself considerable"[66]. Sir George Pearce in his autobiography describes Cook as playing a most active part in Opposition - "he was acquainted with every kind of political strategy and tactics by which the life of a Government can be made miserable. He would stay up for an all night sitting, speak as often and as long as the exigencies of the position required and arrive at the opening of the next session as fresh as a daisy and ready to repeat the performance if required ..... Sir Joseph had the keenest sense of political danger of any member of the Federal Parliament in my experience. When the political sky looked blue and peaceful, he would arrive in cabinet with a gloomy face and tell us of trouble coming, and he was nearly always right". However, Pearce further qualifies his opinion of Cook by adding "such a long apprenticeship to the Opposition to a large extent spoiled him for ministerial and particularly for cabinet work. The habit of criticism never left him and, on the other hand, he had not developed that constructive side which is so essential for both ministerial and cabinet life"[67].

Whatever he may have said privately, Hughes' public valedictory was that Cook 'stood out more than any other man with whom I have been associated as the most reliable and helpful of men. He was a great debater, a dour fighter, and underneath a most lovable personality. I deeply regret his death. The country will mourn his loss. But even though he is gone, the work he did for Australia at a most critical stage of her history still lives"[68]. Some time after Cook's death Malcolm Ellis lured Hughes into a post mortem discussion of him. Asked if he had ever been frightened that Cook might undermine him in the late war years he replied "I was not frightened that he would undermine me. Smother me, yes - but not undermine me ..... but he was loyal, brother, loyal!"[69]

Another critic wrote of Cook - "He has one hobby - Parliament. He lives for nothing else, he knows every rule of the House having broken most of them at times in the heat of a debate and having kept them when the other man broke down. He is always at the table of the House and if he is not there it is of no use looking for him in the billiard room or on the bowling green, he will be found in the library. This faculty it is, of living the parliamentary game, which has put him on top"[70]. Cook was certainly a master of Parliamentary tactics. He may not have been regarded fondly at times by colleagues on the other side of the House but he was certainly someone who had to be taken heed of.

Some may speculate that had Cook remained in England he would not have achieved the success that he did have in Australia. I would tend to agree. But having said that, one has to have regard to the fact that, even prior to meeting his wife, he developed a strong ambition to improve himself. Silverdale may have been the limit of his horizon originally, but I am confident that he would have outgrown that. Furthermore by the time he left for Australia he was already a prominent lay preacher in North Staffordshire, prominent enough for the editor of the <u>Newcastle Guardian</u> to comment that he, together with a Baptist Minister, Rev.W.Bonser, were leaving for Australia - "good men in their respective spheres whom we are to lose"[71]. Furthermore, one should have regard to the fact that, despite the tragic loss of their father at such an early age, Cook's brothers and sisters, who remained in England, all had successful careers. Caroline and Emily, as mentioned earlier, ran a highly successful millinery business at Atherton, Sally (Sarah) became a private nursing sister eventually tending such eminent patients as Sir Winston Churchill, and William had a successful mining career, holding a 1st class certificate in mining[72]. I am confident that had Cook remained in England he certainly would have been successful in some career, but perhaps not as successful as in Australia where there were more opportunities.

Others may speculate that he would not have been so successful without the woman that he married. Although Cook was keen to advance himself, Dame Mary encouraged him from the day he met her as plain Mary Turner. She chose a winner in her husband. Naturally she could not have possibly known, particularly in the early days, that he would at some stage in his career attain the rank of Prime Minister, but nevertheless she realised that he had potential. In some ways she dominated him, she was a very formidable, tough character. But on the other hand she had to be with nine children and her husband frequently away from home on parliamentary business. Quoting her own words she had to be both "father and mother to a young family"[73]. She made life as easy as possible for her husband so that he could concentrate on his career and he gained his strength from her. Their relationship was a strong, practical, loving and secure one[74].

From the moment he arrived in Australia Cook penned long letters to relatives and friends back home in England. He continued to do this even whilst pursuing his political career. Somehow, no matter how busy he was, time would be found for letter writing. Furthermore when he returned to England he never missed an opportunity of visiting relatives or friends, whatever the distance. To some people Cook was much more than a successful politician and public figure. To so many he was a friend, someone who cared and who was very much part of their lives. He cut through the 'special trappings' which surround a public figure, never having lost a genuine modesty[75].

He had no painful reminiscences about the horrors of coalmining in his early days. Once asked if it had been of a disadvantage to him he smiled and replied that "coalmining was an occupation for a philosopher"[76].

In summing up I feel I can do no better than quote the words of Professor Frank Crowley -

"A harsh critic might say that when in office Cook saved the taxpayers money at the expense of the class from which he had risen and when in opposition he was an unprincipled opportunist. On the other hand a sympathetic admirer would say that he was a self made man who rose to the top with those very virtues of hard work, perseverance, self improvement and a sense of duty which formed the central and uplifting message of the Primitive Methodists"[77].

I leave the last word on Cook to John Shenton, his Bible Teacher and friend, who said of him "From the finger tips to the end of his toes he was all polish, but he was genuine and I don't know that I ever met a more genuine man in my life"[78].

Notes

1   <u>The Times</u> 14th Jan 1922

2   <u>Sentinel</u> 16th Jan 1922

3   <u>Ibid</u>

4   <u>The Times</u> 14th Jan 1922

5   <u>Ibid</u> & <u>Sentinel</u> 16th Jan 1922

6   J.Murdoch. <u>op.cit</u>. p.397

7   <u>The Times</u> 14th Jan 1922

8   <u>Ibid</u>

9   J.Murdoch. <u>op.cit</u>. p.402

10   Invitation in Fearnley papers

11   ditto

12   J.Murdoch. <u>op.cit</u>. p.403

13   <u>Ibid</u> p.400

14   Unidentified cutting in Fearnley papers (date confirmed by BBC Archives)

15   Invitations in Fearnley papers

16   <u>Sentinel</u> 13th Nov 1922

17   Ex. info. Mrs.D.Holroyde

18   <u>The Dominions & Independencies of the British Empire</u> ed. H.Gunn. 1924

19   Ex. info. Mrs.J.Fearnley

20   <u>Sydney Morning Herald</u> 22nd May 1924 (there are other unidentified cuttings in the Fearnley papers concerning the launching)

21   Based on cuttings in Fearnley papers

22   <u>Sentinel</u> & <u>London Gazette</u> 3rd June 1925. The <u>Australian Dictionary of Biography</u> & J.Murdoch's thesis incorrectly state that the award was for services to the Red Cross

23   <u>Sentinel</u> 3rd June 1925

24 Service details in Fearnley papers

25 _Sentinel_ 28th April 1926

26 Invitations in Fearnley papers

27 _Woman's Budget_ 5th April 1929

28 Invitations in Fearnley papers

29 Details in Fearnley papers

30 _Perth Daily News_ 20th September 1927

31 J.Murdoch. op.cit. p.403

32 _Testament of Youth_. V.Brittain (19th impression)
    p.393

33 _Ibid_ p.14

34 J.Murdoch. op.cit. p.401

35 _Perth Daily News_ 20th September 1927

36 Court Circular in _The Times_ 10th August 1927

37 Ex. info. Mrs.D.Holroyde

38 _Daily Telegraph_ 20th August 1927

39 _Sunday Times_ 21 August 1927

40 _Daily Telegraph_ 20 August 1927

41 _Perth Daily News_ 20th September 1927

42 This and preceding paragraph based on article on
    'Silchester' contained in _Woman's Budget_ 5th April
    1929

43 J.Murdoch. op.cit. p.405

44 _Ibid_ pp.406/7

45 _The Times_ 14th January 1922 & _Perth Daily News_
    20th September 1927

46 Mrs.M.Wood informed me that one of her greatest
    memories is of her grandfather seeing her son
    Anthony for the first time. Sir Joseph cuddled
    and kissed him, he was so proud of his first great
    grandchild.

47 M.Clark. op.cit. p.207

48   Sydney Morning Herald 29th July 1940

49   Ex. info. Mrs.J.Fearnley

50   Woman's Budget. 5th April 1929

51   Quoted by J.Murdoch. op.cit. p.408

52   Ex. info. Miss C.Morrall

53   Sydney Morning Herald 31 July 1947 and Time
     magazine 11th August 1947

54   The Methodist 9th August 1947

55   Programme of Funeral Service

56   Sentinel 31st July 1947

57   Australian Dictionary of Biography (article on
     Cook)

58   Ex. info. Mrs.M.Wood who also kindly furnished the
     writer with a copy of the script

59   Philatelic Bulletin March 1972

60   J.A. La Nauze. op.cit. p.536

61   J.Murdoch. op.cit. pp.10/11

62   M.H.Ellis. op.cit. pp.20 & 22

63   The Methodist 9th August 1947

64   Ex. info. G.Sawer

65   M.H.Ellis. op.cit. p.21

66   J.A. La Nauze. op.cit. p.536

67   G.F.Pearce. op.cit. p.74

68   Sydney Morning Herald 31st July 1947

69   M.H.Ellis. op.cit. p.21

70   Sentinel 13th January 1922

71   Newcastle Guardian 19th December 1885

72   Ex. info. Mrs.D.Holroyde & Mr.J.Heywood

73   Woman's Budget 5th April 1929

74   Ex. info. Mrs.D.Holroyde

75   Ex. info. Mrs.D.Holroyde

76   M.H.Ellis. op.cit. p.20

77   Australian Dictionary of Biography

78   Sentinel February 1913 (undated) (cutting in
     Sentinel file on Cook)

XXIV   Sir Joseph in the uniform of a Knight Commander of St Michael and St George supported by the Canadian High Commissioner in London at St James' Palace.

Borough of Newcastle-under-Lyme.

TOWN CLERK'S OFFICE,

Newcastle-under-Lyme,

31st August, 1918

Dear Sir,

A Special Meeting of the Council (acting also as the Urban District Council and Burial Board) of this Borough, will be held at the Town Hall, in the said Borough, on **THURSDAY**, the 5th day of September, 1918, at **THREE** o'clock in the afternoon, which Meeting I hereby summon you to attend.

Business :—

For the purpose of conferring the Honorary Freedom of the Borough of Newcastle-under-Lyme upon the Right Honourable Sir Joseph Cook, KCMG

Your obedient Servant,

Joseph Griffith

TOWN CLERK.

TO THE RIGHT HONOURABLE SIR JOSEPH COOK, PC, GCMG,

MINISTER OF STATE FOR THE AUSTRALIAN NAVY

We, the Mayor, Aldermen and Burgesses of the Borough of Newcastle-under-Lyme, on behalf of the inhabitants of the Borough, desire upon the occasion of your visit to this Country as one of the Representatives of the Commonwealth of Australia at the Imperial War Conference now being held, to take the opportunity of offering you our sincerest congratulations upon your successful career, during which you have occupied the very eminent and honourable positions of Prime Minister of the Commonwealth, Minister of Defence and Minister of State for the Australian Navy, and also the offices of Postmaster-General and Minister of Mines and Agriculture of the State of New South Wales. In view of recent events in Europe, we particularly congratulate you upon your foresight and sound statesmanship in having in time of peace exerted yourself to the utmost to place the Naval and Military Forces of the Commonwealth upon a sound and firm basis.

The inhabitants of this District in which you were born, and amongst whom you spent the early days of your life, feel that by your career you have brought honour to the District, and have added another name to the sons of North Staffordshire who have made themselves famous by the pre-eminent services which they have rendered to the Empire.

We hope that your life may be spared for many years during which you may devote your abilities and energies to the promotion of the welfare of the Country of your Adoption and also the County of your Birth.

GIVEN under the Common Seal of the Borough of Newcastle-under-Lyme this Fifth day of September, 1918

W V S GRADWELL GOODWIN, Mayor

J GRIFFITH, Town Clerk.

SFAL

2 Resolved unanimously, upon the Motion of the Mayor seconded by Councillor
M̶ ̶.̶.̶.̶ ̶.̶.̶.̶ ̶ ̶.̶.̶.̶ ̶ ̶pursuance of the Honorary Freedom ̶ ̶.̶.̶.̶

XXV a) Newcastle-under-Lyme Borough Records:
the Mayor's speech on Cook's admission as a Freeman of the Borough.

2 Resolved unanimously upon the Motion of the Mayor seconded by Councillor Mayer —That this Council in pursuance of the Honorary Freedom of Boroughs Act, 1885, do hereby confer upon the Right Hon Sir Joseph Cook P C, G C M G Minister of State for the Australian Navy the Honorary Freedom of the Borough of Newcastle-under-Lyme, and do hereby admit the Right Hon Sir Joseph Cook P C, G C M G, to be an Honorary Freeman of the said Borough

3 Resolved —That the Corporate Seal be affixed to the Address and also the Admission of the Right Hon Sir Joseph Cook P C, G C M G, to the Honorary Freedom of the Borough

4. The Right Hon Sir Joseph Cook, P.C., G C M G signed the Honorary Freemen's Roll and was admitted an Honorary Freeman He then thanked the Corporation for the honour which they had conferred upon him.

General Purposes.

August, 1918 Present, W V S. Gradwell Goodwin, Myott, Councillors Durber, Mayer, ...anis, Whitfield Hodgkinson

Date of Resolution

5 September 19...

forwarded ...

Name and Description of Freeman

Right Honourable Sir Joseph Cook,
G C M G
Minister of the Australian Navy

Signature of Freeman

Joseph Cook

Witnesses to Signature

Gradwell Goodwin Mayor

Joseph Griffith Town Clerk

Bibliography

Unpublished Material

Principally J.Murdoch 'Joseph Cook' (University of New South Wales Ph.D. dissertation) 1968

but also

Chesterton Girl's Board School Log Books

L.Howe 'Causes and consequences of pit disasters in the North Staffordshire Coalfield 1866-1918' (University of Keele B.A. dissertation - Newcastle-under-Lyme Library)

W.B.Nixon - 'The iron industry of the Apedale & Silverdale valleys of North Staffordshire 1768-1901' (Cambridge University B.A. dissertation - Newcastle-under-Lyme Library)

Population Censuses (Enumerators' Returns for Chesterton & Silverdale - various dates)

J.Ravenscroft - 'State, School & Society. The educational environment of Silverdale & Chesterton 1862-1922' (University of Keele B.A. dissertation - Newcastle-under-Lyme Library)

Silverdale County Primary School Log Books

Silverdale St.Lukes School Log Books

Published material

J.Colwell - A century in the Pacific Sydney 1914

M.Clark - A short history of Australia (revised) 1981

Cox's Potteries Annual & Year Book 1923

The County of Stafford and many of its family records W.Pollard & Co. Exeter 1897

F.Crowley - A new history of Australia 1974

B.Dickey - Politics in New South Wales 1856-1900 Melbourne 1969

M.H.Ellis - 'Joseph Cook' in The Bulletin 10th November 1962

R.Gollan - The Coal Miners of New South Wales Melbourne University Press 1963

C.H.Gratton - The Southwest Pacific since 1900
University of Michigan Press 1963

G.Greenwood - Australia - a social & political
history Sydney 1955

H.Gunn - The Dominions & Dependencies of the Empire
Vol.I 1924

Keate's Gazetter & Directory of Staffordshire
(various dates)

C.B.Brassington Knutton (published privately) 1974

J.A.La Nauzé. Alfred Deakin Melbourne University
Press 1966

Newcastle Guardian various dates

B.H.Liddell-Hart - History of the World War 1914-18.
1970

D.Lloyd George - Memoirs of the Peace Conference Yale
University Press 1939

A.W.Martin 'Legislative Assembly of New South Wales
1856-1900' in The Australian Journal of Politics &
History Vol.II 1956

N.Meaney - The search for security in the Pacific
1901-14 Sydney University Press 1981

Newcastle-under-Lyme Borough Council Minutes

H.Nicholson - Peacemaking 1964

J.Niland - 'The birth of the movement for an 8hr.
working day' in The Australian Journal of Politics &
History Vol.XIV 1968

Parish of St.Luke, Silverdale Centenary Brochure
1953

G.F.Pearce - Carpenter to Cabinet 1951

Potteries Examiner various dates

G.H.Reid - My reminiscences 1917

G.Sawer - Australian Federal Politics & Law 1901-29
Melbourne University Press 1972

Silverdale Parish Church Parochial Record Official Handbook and Souvenir of the Grand New Century Bazaar 1901

O.H.K.Spate - <u>Australia</u> 1968

<u>Staffordshire Evening & Weekly Sentinel</u> newspapers

A.J.Taylor - "Coal" in <u>A History of the County of Stafford</u> Vol.II ed. M.W.Greensdale & J.G.Jenkins 1967

ENVOIE

XXVIII   Sir Joseph and Lady Cook in happy retirement.